Rites of Raven's Knoll

edited by

Juniper Birch

Austin Lawrence

Gypsy Birch

Dr. Maryanne Pearce

ISBN-13: 978-1535183055
ISBN-10: 1535183055

For the Ancestors, the Gods, the Spirits, and the Land.

CONTENTS

ACKNOWLEDGMENTS

Foremost thanks goes to the numerous folk that contributed their creativity, emotions, secret insights, artistry, and spirit to assembling a collage of the sacred, a window into Raven's Knoll. Submissions for this book were received in 2014.

The editors would like to congratulate each other for finally completing this overdue project: Juniper Birch connected with Pagan community members far and wide to encourage and nurture their contributions to this volume; Austin Lawrence drummed up interest, arranged and formatted copy; while Gypsy Birch and Maryanne Pearce also proofed and copy edited.

The cover illustration is the work of the Ottawa artist Krista Schmidt. Krista is a new, but annual, visitor to the Knoll. Her work has graced the covers of programs for both the Witches' Sabbat at Raven's Knoll and Kaleidoscope Gathering. The image on this book first appeared on the cover of the Kaleidoscope Gathering 2016 program, which was created to express the theme of "Portals." You can often find her at Knoll events, where she can be found trading the hustle of mundane life for one of community, spirituality, and nature.

Austin (Auz) Lawrence

RAVEN'S KNOLL: A CREATION STORY

by Maryanne Pearce

After 17 years of organization, Pamela Fletcher asked Austin Lawrence and I to take over the Kaleidoscope Gathering (KG) so that she could retire. It was 2007 when we first started talking about it, 2008 when we agreed, and 2009 when it was announced first to staff in March and at KG to the community. KG 2010 would be under a change of management – and on new, Pagan-owned land.

The idea of having permanent, Pagan-owned land had been discussed for many years. In the ten years before Raven's Knoll was created, many KG staff had gone to see possible sites, looked into options for buying land, all to no avail. With Pam's request for us to take over KG, the idea needed to be revisited. No one knew better than Austin and I how much work it took to put KG together – both before and during the event. While we thought about taking on this huge task, we wondered about how we could ensure that the money from Pagans went back into improvements and expansions for future Pagan events. Of course, we still had no idea what we were getting ourselves into.

Austin and I spoke to our bank and received very general information and a "sure, no problem" kind of response. We would need to refinance our house and get a business loan. We began looking at the on-line listings for real estate. Our locations were ideally within two hours of Ottawa, hopefully somewhere halfway between Montreal and Toronto. There were only a few campgrounds listed – and they were all well over what we could possibly consider. We had no idea how much we could "afford" but we knew the million dollar range was not it!

I was looking at the real estate listings one night and got lost online. I thought I was looking in the Perth area. I had started looking for residential or farm land of 100 acres or more. I had opened up a listing and started looking through the descriptions and photos. There was a photo of a building with a sign saying "laundry". Huh? I kept looking through this listing and more and more photos suggested I was looking at a campground – an ice machine, a "party shack". Nothing on the listing said this is what it was though. I called Austin. And the next day, I called the realtor.

The property at 10441 Highway 60, Eganville, was indeed an old campground but was listed as residential and was being sold as such. It had been known as "Idle Hours" since about 1970. In 1998, it had been purchased and continued as a campground. In that purchase, the original owners severed the property, taking three acres off with the main house. The trailer that acted as the main house of the campground, the cabin, all the outbuildings, the well, and all of the rest of the 100 acre campground made up the new Idle Hours. In 2000, the owners opened a riding school called Pine Grove Stables. The entire operation closed in 2003 due to needed upgrades and the owners' children leaving for university. They had tried to sell the property several times. One problem that had arisen is that residential properties can only mortgage the first five acres – which severely limited the pool of available buyers.

We could not see the property in the winter of 2009 because the snow would have prevented us from seeing the land as we would need to do to confirm its suitability. At the March 2009 staff meeting, however, after the announcement of Pam's retirement for the 2010 festival year, we showed everyone the photos. There was a collective sense that we had found our new home.

During the time we were waiting to go see the land, we had been considering names. Much like trying to name a child or pet, there are so many choices, so much history you want to include. I got an email from Austin one morning. A name – perhaps better described as a vision – had come to him. The name? "Raven's Knoll of Wisdom Whence Flows Rivers of Hazel-Fed Salmon-y Knowledge Through Verdant Groves of Ancient Ash and Thorn From Silent Wells of Elder Days by the Longhouse Hearth of Glowing Friendship". I discovered this was too long for government forms; "Raven's Knoll" would have to suffice.

In was April before we could go see the land. There was still snow on the ground when Austin and I, along with Pam and David Rolfe, first drove in the neighbours' drive way. Our first thought was that this could not work; the neighbours shared a drive way during the winter and the houses were as close together as in a suburb. We shook our heads in dismay. But, we were there; we might as well walk below and see the rest of the property.

We walked down along the fence line between the property and Frontier Trails Kids Camp next door. We walked down behind the (then) small trees that now shelter the Spiral, and what we now call the Telephone Tree Forest and Mirkwood. We came across the Gnome Home; it had no gnomes but we could sense the spirits. And then we found the Rainbow Tree.

We walked into the campground area, circled around, and came to the river which was swollen and overflowing its banks. Pam squealed and hugged a tree. Her hands on the ground, she declared "you can feel the drums below the Earth waiting for us". I think the realtor knew they had us then.

Then the business of starting a business began. Raven's Knoll (RK) and the KG Festival had been incorporated separately in the spring of 2010 through a lawyer. I had prepared two long business plans: one for KG, one for RK. Our bank's business manager was completely useless, despite his earlier assurances. I went to other banks and was either stonewalled, ignored, or the same message was repeated: this sounds like a hobby, not a religious endeavour or a business. That made me furious.

I ended up going to the main branch of Scotiabank, our bank. I walked in without an appointment, was seen by a small business advisor right away, and presented the plans. Krista English, the banker, called me within a day: everything looked fine to her except that one financial document needed to be redone. I handed in the revised package the following day and things were underway! There were inspections and hurdles and paperwork. I didn't work on my doctoral thesis much during this time; paperwork is my domain and I was determined.

In order to ensure that the property was as it was described, the banker needed to attend the property in person. I took the day off work and we drove up separately. As we drove through the drive way (not the neighbours' drive), there was a raven on either side, on the knolls that we had discovered were on the property entrance. The banker was quite startled by this – it seemed a little spooky to her. I had a giant sense of relief and contentment. We walked the land together. She was as excited as Pam had been. She became our advocate to make Raven's Knoll a reality.

It all was coming together. Our offer had been accepted after going back and forth, and over a competing bid from a neighbour. Again, that five acre mortgage rule came into play. As a business, we were not subjected to that provision. The property and pages of chattels were included, and were to be ours on August 19, 2009.

We came again, with staff and other members of the Pagan community in June and July. The announcement was made at KG 2009, and an Open House was set for September, one month after taking possession of the land.

All members of the KG staff, as well as some other Pagan people who were able to spend a week at RK, came to assist with moving in and taking the land that hot day in August.

The well on the property became our Sacred Well. A circle dug in the middle of a field, hidden by small bushes; it was a quiet and lovely place. It was our first sacred site, and used that very weekend in our land-taking ritual.

Everyone gathered at the Well. Doug Thew, Sarita, Shane Hultquist and Brendan Roche stood on guard outside of the circle: the outsiders. The rest of us gathered in ritual. Austin sacrificed a sword and scabbard into the dark waters of the Well. I offered gifts of sage, cedar, sweetgrass, and tobacco to the Ancestors and Spirits of the land, giving honour to the Algonquin people and land on which we stood. As we finished, someone noticed a rainbow. As we stood in silent awe of a huge, bright rainbow that seemed to begin on the land and end in the Well, a second, fully visible rainbow appeared above it. The brightest double rainbow I have ever seen.

The public land-taking was held a month later at the Open House. That was the first ritual done in what is now known as the Raven Field. Austin had a cracker wheel and he broke these upon the rock altar. I was to place the sweetgrass and the seasonal root vegetables upon the altar. However, inspiration, the voice of the Gods or sheer lunacy overtook me. Instead, I attempted to split a squash over the pointy rock. I am not very strong to begin with, and crackers smash a lot easier than do squash. My skin, however, opened easily. Marie the Medic and Pam were watching me drip blood all over the altar during the ritual, and Marie patched me up afterwards. The land, it seems, wanted a blood sacrifice as I was honouring the land and spirits. Maybe it is because I am part Mohawk on Algonquin land. Or because I am inept at smashing vegetables. Whatever the reason, Raven's Knoll was sanctified and blessed.

And so the adventure really began!

Maryanne Pearce, also known as MA, is one of the Stewards of Raven's Knoll and a co-organizer of the Kaleidoscope Gathering. She holds a doctorate in law, focusing on missing and murdered vulnerable women. Her Master's thesis in Anthropology focused on the Canadian Pagan community. MA is in charge of all the paper involved with RK and KG. She lives in Ottawa with her husband Austin Lawrence, her two adult children Kadri Rainne and Joven Wolf, and various four legged friends.

OPEN HOUSE RITUAL

by Maryanne Pearce, Austin Lawrence, and friends

This was the first public ritual performed at Raven's Knoll, where the broader Pagan community first met together on the land. Maryanne served as the Priestess and Austin as the Priest.

As a pan-Pagan ritual, it follows a familiar Wiccan format, with some modifications to accommodate other Pagan paths. As is the norm for the ceremonial culture of those associated with the Kaleidoscope Gathering, the ritual includes doses of solemnity, frivolity, and radical inclusivity, in equal measure.

- - - - - - - - - - ~ - - - - - - - - - -

Gathering

Cryers call the folk together for the ritual.

Priestess .... Welcome everyone … community, the harvest, this land. Austin and I wish to thank you, each and every one of you, for being here, for witnessing the birth of the community dream of a land base for Pagans, and for joining with us today in this ritual.

Priest .... In this rite we will join together in a sacred circle to invoke the spirits of this place and our Gods and Goddesses to join us in celebration of our ability to come together in community. In this ritual we will honour our Gods with an offering of the seasons fruits and receive their blessings through the sprinkling of the Waters of Life straight from the horn.

Cast Circle

Priest .... We make holy this sacred place by carrying the light of the sun to mark the turning of the season and the light of wisdom that we can each find within.

Caster carries a candle lantern around the circle clockwise.

Priestess .... This place, Raven's Knoll, is a dream of community, our community. For we are all different, but come together as one, to experience the Divine in ourselves, in each other and in nature.

Chantress .. *Someone who can actually hold a tune leads the group in a rendition of the Wiccan chant "We Are a Circle".*

Call Quarters

Officiates at the East, South, West and North call the quarters in the manner of their tradition, as they see fit.

Invocation of Spirits and Raven

Priestess .... *In an extemporaneous manner the Priestess describes the spirit and symbol of the Raven; highlighting how many peoples honour them:*

The Raven is an important symbol in many Elder cultures. Amongst many First Nations peoples Raven is a well-known trickster and creator figure. His trials and tribulations helped to create the world and serve as an example of how we should behave in it. In ancient Norse belief the All-Father God Odin sends his two ravens – Thought and Memory – out into the world each day where they represent our connection to the Gods through our very consciousness. In ancient Celtic belief Ravens can represent a people's connection to their land and in some later folk belief ravens served as familiars whereby the spirits of the Ancestors can speak to the living.

A Handmaiden lights sage and cedar incense.

Priestess .... I call on you Raven to bring us the wisdom of merriment and mirth, and lessons well won. Here is a gift of tobacco and the Three Sisters. All my relations.

Priestess offers tobacco and beans and corn and squash.

Priest .... On behalf of those here I call on the Spirits of this land, all hidden folk and forest dwellers. Oh – River Bonnechere, Valley Highlands, Fen and Field, Forest and Sacred Well – wights who dwell here and there – come to us for we honour you. Here is a gift of sunwheel bread and nine silver coins. Hail!

Priest offers wheel bread and nine silver coins.

Invocation of Gods and Goddesses

Priest .... We are many paths, who honour many Goddesses and Gods. To all of them we ask that they join us. We will do this through energy of our voices and souls.

Priestess .... Let us draw to us the power of our Goddesses in three chants of "Mah."

The Chantress leads the group in a free flowing tonal chant.

Priest .... Lets us drawn to us the power of our Gods in three chants of "Ohm."

The Chantress leads the group in a free flowing tonal chant.

Priest .... Oh Gods and Goddesses of the folk present here. We honour you, we rejoice that you walk amongst us. We ask that you grant us your aspects to bring us luck and victory in our lives.

Priest does the hammer sign over the horn; Priestess brings the horn to her forehead, to her lips and to her heart.

Horn-bearer moves clockwise around the circle asperging people's hands with the water using cedar branches, after first doing so for the Priestess and Priest. They keep circulating until everyone is covered, throughout the rest of the ritual.

Priestess .... On behalf of the people here we offer you the fruits of the season.

Handmaiden places the first fruits on the altar.

(Editors' Note: At this point, please refer to the previous chapter for the story of "the

accidental blood sacrifice" by Maryanne.)

Priest .... Let us give voice to our joy in living, to the gifts the Gods bring ... *(extemporaneous words)* ... by raising our individual voices as one voice, three times. Repeat after me. Hail! Hail! Hail!

Handmaiden pours out a secondary horn on the altar.

Working

Priestess .... We stand in this circle before each other, before the Spirits and before the Gods. We are a diverse group of people, which gives us strength and makes life interesting. We look to each other and see differences, but we also see what is the same.

Priest .... Our work today will be simple. We will announce to the Universe that we are here. We will make ten calls, each representing a different element of our community. We cannot call all groups, but know that these calls represent everyone. Please respond "We are!!" at whichever and every call the spirit moves you.

Priest .... The Gods and Goddesses of this land wish to know who has come, who will stay, and who will build and sustain this land that is Raven's Knoll.

Alternating, Priestess and Priest shout for the call and response. The Cryer leads every response to get the timing right.

Priestess .... The Ancestors of this land wish to know to know who has come, who will stay, and who will build and sustain this land that is Raven's Knoll.

> Are Pagans here? We are!!!
> Are Wizards here? We are!!!
> Are Children of the Rainbow here? We are!!!
> Are Seekers here? We are!!!
> Are Shamans here? We are!!!
> Are Heathens here? We are!!!
> Are Pirates here? We ARRRRR!!!
> Are Druids here? We are!!!
> Are Witches here? We are!!!
> Are those-without-labels, but happy to be among us, here? We

are!!!!

(As the calls were made, people spontaneously started to run into the middle of the circle for a group hug, with much laughing, shouting, and falling over. It was general, joyous mayhem with a pile of people forming and then being unwound into their individual forms again.)

Priest .... [*Breathing, using exaggerated gestures.*] Let us now drink deeply of the power we have raised through nine deep breaths, connecting us to all of the worlds and deep into the earth.

Dissolve Circle

Priestess .... This ceremony is ended now, but the circle will not be unbroken, nor the Gods and Spirits gone. Their energy remains to flow through all the rites and magick to take place on this land in the future. Let us let the energy we have raised meld into the Holy Mother Earth as we chant together…

Chantress .. *Someone who can actually hold a tune leads the group in a rendition of the Wiccan chant "Merry Meet Again".*

Maryanne Pearce, also known as MA, is one of the Stewards of Raven's Knoll and a co-organizer of the Kaleidoscope Gathering. She holds a doctorate in law, focusing on missing and murdered vulnerable women. Her Master's thesis in Anthropology focused on the Canadian Pagan community. MA is in charge of all the paper involved with RK and KG. She lives in Ottawa with her husband Austin Lawrence, her two adult children Kadri Rainne and Joven Wolf, and various four legged friends.

Austin Lawrence is known in the Pagan community as "Auz." He is one of the Stewards of Raven's Knoll and a co-organizer of the Kaleidoscope Gathering. Auz has a Master's degree in Anthropology and is a Heathen who is an oathed Goði that serves as the Keeper of the Raven's Knoll Vé. Auz is also a former Stag King of the Kaleidoscope Gathering. He lives in Ottawa with his wife Maryanne Pearce, his two adult children Kadri Rainne and Joven Wolf, and a menagerie of family pets.

THE VÉ AND THE BLÓT TO ODIN

by Austin Lawrence and Erik Lacharity

Introduction

Raven's Knoll was established to serve people from a wide array of different Pagan communities. A significant number of these folk identify as Heathen or Ásatrú, or are interested in those spiritual practices. Heathenry is the practice of traditions collectively associated with the religious and spiritual beliefs of the pre-Christian Germanic and Scandinavian peoples. Ásatrú is the name given to the religion commonly practiced by the speakers of Old Norse during the Viking Age, and which is now again practiced by modern communities of adherents around the globe.

In 2012, at the Hail and Horn Gathering, a sacred place of worship was established at Raven's Knoll for honouring the Gods and Goddesses of Heathenry and Ásatrú. For the first time in Canada (to our knowledge) there is a public place of worship set aside for the worship of the pre-Christian Scandinavian and Germanic holy powers.

The Vé (pronounced "Vay") that was established is a holy place, a home for our Gods in Miðgarð.[i] It is a frith-yard; a place set aside, a place of peace and good thoughts. In the religious custom of the Heathens that visit Raven's Knoll, the location is holy and must always be respected. When it has been sanctified and made sacred by the ritual of hanging the vé-bond rope, everything in it and everything that takes place there is considered to be particularly holy.

The practice we have established for religious ritual and spiritual engagement at the Raven's Knoll Vé is grounded in historical research drawn from Viking Age Scandinavia, continental Germania, and points east in Rus-land where historical Heathens traveled.

The Vé in the Context of Heathen Holy Sites

> While unfenced areas and natural features of the landscape might be regarded as holy places, the need to provide an enclosed space, a temenos or sacred precinct, was often felt. It might enclose figures of the gods or sacred objects, or provide an obvious boundary around holy ground, separating it either temporarily or permanently from the normal world. Examples of this from the Viking Age ... are the ropes enclosing a court of law, the careful marking out of the area in which an official duel was fought, the squares on the floor used by a wizard calling up the dead, and the stone settings placed round graves (Ellis-Davidson, 27).

The most ancient sites for religious worship were "in the open air, in holy groves and meadows, before rocks and hillocks, or on the shores of swampy lakes into which offerings were cast" (Simpson, 1969: 180). Amongst the Indo-Europeans, generally, but specifically amongst the ...

> ... Celts and Germans there seem originally to have been few permanent and elaborate temples used as meeting places for worship and sacrifice. In spite of the rigors of the climate, the place where men sought contact with the supernatural powers was for the most part in the open air. The resorting to holy places was something which could be witnessed by outside observers, often arousing interest and curiosity. This in the works of Greek and Latin writers we hear repeatedly of sacred woods and groves, sanctuaries in forest clearings and on hilltops, beside springs and lakes and on islands, and of places set apart for the burial of the noble dead (Ellis-Davidson, 1988: 13).

Tacitus, the Roman senator and historian, wrote of the Germanic peoples (Tacitus, 1970) in the first century C.E. in his history *Germania* that they did not erect images of their Gods or build temples:

> The Germans, however, do not consider it consistent with the grandeur of celestial beings to confine the gods within walls, or to liken them to the form of any human countenance. They consecrate woods and groves, and they apply the names of deities to that hidden presence which is seen only by the eye of reverence.

After the Migration Period (376 to 793 C.E.) and into the Viking Age (793 to 1066 C.E.), cultural contact with other Pagan peoples who did erect temples and create other sacred precincts increased. Especially in the Viking Age, interactions and contacts with various Christian traditions, which focused their worship within sacred buildings, was common. Probably as a reaction to the religious practices of their neighbours, over time religious worship at wild places of significance with no created images of the Gods was augmented (but not supplanted) by worship involving simple images of the Gods in outdoor areas modified by human intervention and then more commonly in buildings made sacred which housed more ornate representations of the Gods.

The name that is now most commonly given to the simple outdoor sacred space created for Heathen worship is the *vé* (in Old Norse, alternatively a *wēoh*, in Old English). The word itself derives from the Common Germanic term **wīha* meaning sacred or holy. Its use is attested to in skaldic and mythological poetry (Simek, 1993). At its most basic the vé was an open space marked off by light barriers, such as posts and ropes or wattle fencing. In some locations in South Scandinavia during the late Viking Age, a particular form of large vé, formed in the shape of a "V" seems to have evolved (Simpson, 1967). However, it is clear from literary sources that the term vé applied to a wide array of shrine or worship locations types and forms, so long as they were enclosed and without a roof (Simek, 1993).

A commonplace name element in Old Norse is *hov* and in Old Norwegian *hof,* both of which denote a Heathen shrine. Scholars, however, do not believe it likely that all of the hof names originally meant "temple" or "shrine", rather most would have referred to a small building or area of a farmstead devoted to Heathen worship. There is no evidence of buildings used solely as Pagan temples being widespread in Scandinavia. As almost all of the places with names compounded in "hof" are actually farmsteads, an original meaning along the lines of "farm where cult meetings were held by the locals" might be more appropriate (Sproston).

Certainly, temples with "special enclosures" were known among the Pagan Anglo-Saxons, as is shown in the Venerable Bede's *Ecclesiastical History of the English Nation*, Book II, Section XIII:

> ... I advise, O king, that we instantly abjure and set fire to those temples and altars which we have consecrated without reaping any benefit from them." In short, the king publicly gave his license to Paulinus to preach the Gospel, and renouncing idolatry, declared that he received the faith of Christ: and then he inquired of the high priest who should first profane the altars and temples of their idols, with the enclosures that were

about them.... This place where the idols were is still shown, not far from York, to the eastward, beyond the river Derwent, and is now called Godmundingham, where the high priest, by the inspiration of the true God, profaned and destroyed the altars which he had himself consecrated.

The way historic Heathen societies managed the building and upkeep of holy places and shrines is not clear, as textual sources are virtually non-existent and archeology is mute on the point. There is some evidence from the Iceland sagas for how the institutions of hofs were managed. For instance, from the *Eyrbyggja Saga* there is this description of Thorolf Mosturskeggi's hof (Anonymous, 1989):

Around the pedestal in this side room were arranged the images of the gods. Everyone was to pay a contribution to the temple .... On his part, the goði had to maintain the temple at his own expense, so that it did not deteriorate and hold the sacrificial banquets in it.

The later church-farms that the hofs evolved into after the conversion indicates that these locations of religious observance were established on privately-held land managed by the land-holder, but that the surrounding and connected community that worshipped together at the location contributed to its construction and upkeep (Bycock, 2001; Lucas, 2009). Presumably, the vés and similar shrines were similarly organized, but required less investment of resources or concentration of capital and political power to maintain.

Establishing the Raven's Knoll Vé

As we see, much of the evidence in the lore indicated that historic Heathens had special places to meet the Gods in this life. After the establishment of Raven's Knoll by Austin Lawrence and Maryanne Pearce, the Canadian Pagan and Heathen community had a home, a place of community to build the infrastructure they required for gatherings and worship. Given Austin's close relationship with the traditions of Old Norse religion and wish to give life again to the old ways of honouring the Gods, it was natural that an effort be made to worship as of old. There was not enough capital yet in the community to invest in the building of a hof, but there was a wish to demonstrate sincere efforts to reconstruct our ancient faith. Thus, we settled upon the establishment of a vé.

We were inspired by the most detailed textual account of worship at a vé-like location by historic Heathens. In 921 C.E., a Muslim named Ibn

Fadlan was sent by the Caliph of Baghdad on an embassy to the King of the Bulgars of the Middle Volga. He wrote an account of his travels called a *risala*. This risala is one of the only first-person accounts of the Heathen people, the Rus, the majority of whom were born in the area we now know as Sweden. In this part of Ibn Fadlan's account he describes a religious observance of the Rus (Viking Answer Lady, 2014a):

> When the ships come to this mooring place, everybody goes ashore with bread, meat, onions, milk and intoxicating drink and betakes himself to a long upright piece of wood that has a face like a man's and is surrounded by little figures, behind which are long stakes in the ground. The Rus prostrates himself before the big carving and says, "O my Lord, I have come from a far land and have with me such and such a number of slave girls and such and such a number of sables," and he proceeds to enumerate all his other wares. Then he says, "I have brought you these gifts," and lays down what he has brought with him, and continues, "I wish that you would send me a merchant with many dinars and dirhems,[ii] who will buy from me whatever I wish and will not dispute anything I say." Then he goes away.
>
> If he has difficulty selling his wares and his stay is prolonged, he will return with a gift a second or third time. If he has still further difficulty, he will bring a gift to all the little idols and ask their intercession, saying, "These are the wives of our Lord and his daughters and sons." And he addresses each idol in turn, asking intercession and praying humbly. Often the selling goes more easily and after selling out he says, "My Lord has satisfied my desires; I must repay him," and he takes a certain number of sheep or cattle and slaughters them, gives part of the meat as alms, brings the rest and deposits it before the great idol and the little idols around it, and suspends the heads of the cattle or sheep on the stakes. In the night, dogs come and eat all, but the one who has made the offering says, "Truly, my Lord is content with me and has consumed the present I brought him."

The Vé we built was inspired by ancient sources, but was also a product of pragmatism and modern imagination. The enclosure itself is set in a clearing in the forest, surrounded by hawthorn trees, and further around by the mixed temperate forest of this part of Canada. It is in an out-of-the-way corner of the 100 acres of Raven's Knoll, sited so that regular campers do not accidentally profane it and worshippers will not be disturbed. Importantly, most sacred sites at Raven's Knoll are designed to be multi-use for different religious traditions, while this one is not. Thus, it was felt more polite to site it in areas that were not so intensively multi-use.

Inside the natural enclosure of the thorn trees, a large rectangle roughly on a North-South axis was laid out. This orientation was selected so that the God-poles would feel the rising sun on their faces in the morning, with some later euhemerised lore indicating that the Æsir came from the East (Sturluson, 2005). Kevin McLaughlin assisted Austin in this phase of construction. The post holes were dug using the Raven's Knoll tractor, named Duchess. Nine logs of six feet in length were cut of red pine harvested from the land, and the bottoms were flamed to resist rot. Austin made offerings of ale, cream, and red ochre before each of the posts were set, using words inspired by some of the liturgy of Raven Kindred North in Massachusetts (Raven Kindred North, 2014). Posts were spaced at the corners and in the middle of each side, with the ninth post added on the North-East corner to form a doorway into the Vé. The enclosed space is about 50 feet on the long West and East sides and 25 feet on the other sides.

The last remaining large stones from the very sandy ground of Raven's Knoll were used to create an altar space, called a *hörg*, on the West side of the vé. Many of the largest stones were donated by David Rolfe from the land where he grew up on Haliburton, Ontario. Gypsy Birch assisted Austin with creating the hörg. The hörg is a pile of stones with a large flat stone on top, roughly created to resemble a dolmen with a covered front side. After construction, the hörg was wetted with mead and three silver coins provided as an offering. The hörg was centrally placed so that a shallow semi-circle of God-poles can be installed about two feet apart spanning from the middle of the South side to the middle of the North side. The poles started to be set directly behind the hörg, on the West side. This created a space where all the God-poles, which stand about 12 feet out of the ground, face in towards the people gathered in front of the hörg on the central-East side of the enclosure.

The Vé is only considered holy though, when the vé-bond rope is hung upon the nine marker posts. The sacred importance of this rope is evidenced long after the use of vé had given way to worship in temples, such as the golden chain that hung around the grand temple at Uppsala (Adam of Bremen, 2002). The nine posts stand rooted in the ground, one for each of the Nine Worlds, to hold the vé-bond rope. True hemp cordage or horse hair rope in the thickness and lengths required proved to be too expensive and time consuming to obtain, so we used a jute-hemp rope instead.

The entrance path winds through a field, through a dark swale in the forest, rising through a hawthorn grove, to meet the Vé from the north. Facing the entering folk is a wonderful carved and painted runestone three feet tall. It was carved by Andy Biggers in commemoration of Austin's study of the Old Norse religious tradition, his actions in leading rituals and forging Heathen community bonds, and his Goði oath. It serves Austin as reminder of his responsibilities and obligations to the Vé and the people so served, and it is a beautiful and wonderful aesthetic piece of art. Another smaller runestone, gifted through bonds of frith by Sean Feeny Bastien of Nine Mountains Kindred, has joined it there.

Behaviour in the Frith-Yard

There are two important attitudes that characterize worship within a vé: a lack of conflict, and the display of respect. The Vé is viewed as a home for the Gods, deserving of honour, and is a place that should be free from strife.

Even in earlier Heathen times, when images of the Gods were not commonly displayed in the sacred enclosure, the strictures of frith and respect were central to worship at holy sites. Tacitus provides an example in *Germania* of how worship occurred at the sacred grove of the Semnones tribe:

> Of all the Suevians, the Semnones recount themselves to be the most ancient and most noble. The belief of their antiquity is confirmed by religious mysteries. At a stated time of the year, all the several people descended from the same stock, assemble by their deputies in a wood; consecrated by the idolatries of their forefathers, and by superstitious awe in times of old. There by publicly sacrificing a man, they begin the horrible solemnity of their barbarian worship. To this grove another sort of reverence is also paid. No one enters it otherwise than bound with ligatures, thence professing his subordination and meanness, and the power of the Deity there. If he fall down, he is not permitted to rise or be raised, but grovels along upon the ground. And of all their superstition, this is the drift and tendency; that from this place the nation drew their original, that here their god, the supreme governor of the world, resides, and that all things else whatsoever are subject to him and bound to obey him.

Thus, the holy place is a site in which not only are no weapons borne, but no hand can be raised in violence because the hands are bound. This attitude of extreme respect and sense of subservience when taking part in worshipping directly in the presence of the Gods is one that has informed religious practice at the Raven's Knoll Vé.

Other examples from a later period in Iceland can be found in the Eyrbyggja Saga (Anonymous, 1989) where Thorolf Mosturskeggi specified taboos surrounding the holy site, Helgafell Mountain. At this natural place of worship, "nothing was to be killed on this mountain, neither cattle nor human beings, except those cattle which left there of their own accord," and further "no man should look upon it unwashed". The place must not be defiled in any way whatsoever, neither through bloodshed nor human excrement. If someone had to relieve themselves, "a skerry was set aside which was called Dirtskerry". This rule of abhorrence of bloodshed and filth in the presence of the Gods is another piece of the lore that has informed religious practice at the Raven's Knoll Vé

The Vé is a holy place that is a place of *frith*. Frith is an important concept in Heathen religion. It is a term meaning something akin to peace, but a peace created by compromise and social relationships not by a lack of conflict or the simple application of the principle of forgiveness. It has strong associations with the ideas of security and stability. A vé is also called a *friðgarðar*. A *garð* and its related terms have the meaning of an enclosed yard, a hedge or fence that encloses, or a delineated region or 'world' (e.g., similar in meaning to "the land of X"). In Old English the same word, *friþgeard*, was translated in Christian times as place of asylum or sanctuary. The religious concepts of historic Heathen peoples can also be observed in the rituals surrounding their practice of law:

> Law-courts and other areas in which law-related activities took place in the Viking Age were commonly marked out with hazel poles (höslur) and "holy ropes" (vé-bond, "sacred bonds") and like religious spaces so marked, they were considered to be friðgarðar or "peace-enclosures," in which no weapons could be drawn.

> Originally, a Þing was to some extent a religious gathering, "hallowed" in the name of the gods, and the peace which all must keep during the lawsuits and debates was akin to the peace surrounding a sanctuary [vé] (Simpson, 1967 in Viking Answer Lady, 2014b).

Thus, a vé is a holy place where through religious ritual frith is created, frith is enacted, and where frith can be sought.

To enter and participate in any ritual taking place in the Raven's Knoll Vé, three basic rules should be strictly followed as a sign of respect for the holy powers and to ensure one's own continued good fortune.

1. Honour only the Æsir

- Honour and speak of only the Gods and Goddesses of the Æsir and Vanir (e.g., Thor and Frigg, Frey and Freya) or their clear allies (e.g., Aegir and Ran), and those bound in loyalty to them by blood-oath (e.g., Loki) within this vé.
- Wights that stand in opposition to the Gods (e.g., Fenrir, Hel, Thiazi) should not be honoured within this enclosure.
- Gods, Goddesses, or Spirits of other pantheons or monotheistic faiths should not be honoured in the holy enclosure (e.g., Diana, Cernunnos, Jesus, Baron Samedi, Lakshimi).
- This must be demonstrated in word and action. Thus, do not wear signs or symbols of Gods, Goddess, or Spirits not of this Heathen custom. (Tattoos are okay, since they are part of you.)

2. Keep frith

- Maintain peaceful and socially harmonious relations in your actions and deeds between people and Gods and Spirits.
- Carry nothing that might be considered a weapon into the Vé.
- Tools to be used to maintain the sacred enclosure and certain items to be explicitly used as part of a ritual to honour the Gods may, in some circumstances, enter the sacred grounds (e.g., hammer, wood carving knife, ritual spear). Check with a goði or gythia who has previously performed public services in the Raven's Knoll Vé before bearing such items before the Gods.
- Do not insult people or Gods within the Vé, even in jest.

3. Maintain sacral cleanliness

- Let no human bodily excretions touch the ground or any object in the Vé.
- Definitely do not allow any spittle, urine, or feces to come in contact with the sacred area.
- Avoid contact with earwax, tears, sweat, pus, and blood, if possible. If emotion, medical necessity, or extreme youth prevent one from following this taboo, it is understood that some contact may occur and is considered permissible.

- Refrain from personal self-care (e.g., blowing your nose, spitting out a bug, applying bug spray or sunscreen) in the Vé. Simply leave the Vé completely to do so.

After discussions between people using the Vé, we have added the tradition of not bringing electronic equipment into the enclosure unless required. (This also serves to remind people to turn off their cell phones during ritual!) A 'weapons-rack' with a shelf has been constructed just outside of the Vé upon which to place, hang, or rest any items that are not being taken into the holy grounds.

The Hail and Horn Gathering

It was an evening in November of 2011 when Austin, the Goði of Raven's Knoll, sent an email to Erik Lacharity of Rúnatýr Kindred, seeking rede[iii] from Runatyr's Lawspeaker. In short, the email was somewhat mysterious in nature, stating that: "I was mulling over the start of an idea that I think you and your kin might be interested in."[iv] Shortly after, Austin met with the members of Rúnatýr Kindred at Rúnamoot[v] and presented his idea, which would see the formation of an ongoing Heathen gathering at the site of Raven's Knoll, aided and informed by members of Rúnatýr Kindred and other local and distant Heathens, each giving input on how the gathering should be formed and maintained in the years to come; a gathering of the folk, for the folk, by the folk.

In early 2012, discussions were underway between members of Raven's Knoll, Runatyr Kindred, and many others as to what this gathering would be called. What would be its stated purpose? Which needs of the greater Heathen communities should be met? A series of exchanges took place between the two lead organizers to determine the answers to those questions. It's all well and good to want to establish a gathering, but a gathering will never be maintained if it is but for the sake of gathering.

As a starting point, it was decided that the new gathering, as of then still nameless, needed a primary historical foundation, a layer of ancestral lore upon which a modern superstructure could be framed and eventually furnished. Through mutual agreement, that initial cornerstone would be the described account of Ibn Fadlan in which it is said: "[everybody]… betakes himself to a long upright piece of wood that has a face like a man's…". Therefore, the erecting of God-poles would be that starting point and as such create a literal placement of axis mundi to bind the folk.

It was decided that the name of the gathering would be the "Hail and Horn Gathering" (HHG), and that the foundation and purpose of HHG would two-fold and would be 'from the Well:'[vi]. Hail – the forging of a deep relationship with the Gods, and Horn – building bonds and maintaining bonds with other Heathens. These would be exemplified by a tripartite ritual beginning at the onset of the gathering and ending upon the last day, consisting of *blót*, *húsel*, and *symbel*. This format ensures that the entire weekend is holy, not just at certain times of the day, such as when specific rituals are underway. There are obviously times when the holiness of the event gains a more sacral nature, such as during the blót, húsel and to a degree, symbel.

Blót, in the context of HHG, consists of a the raising of a God-pole and the making of sacrifice as consistent with and reconstructed from the accounts of Ahmad ibn Fadlān among the Rus and bolstered by Icelandic, Scandinavian, Old English, and Continental sources where appropriate and fitting. Húsel, in the context of HHG, consists of a sacral meal shared between humankind and the Gods with a format inspired by Old English accounts and developed further with experimentation, evolving with each year. Symbel, in the context of HHG, consists of a "High Symbel," meaning a 'modern' symbel which is as close to the historical sources as can be achieved, most specifically Old English, devoid of any non-Germanic influences where deemed appropriate by the Symbel Leader. The exact format of such is fluid within its parameters and is subject to evolving over time based upon input by the folk. (For more on Symbel see Pollington, 2003.)

The organizers then formulated a strategy which would bring about *weal* to those who would attend. As Goði of Raven's Knoll, weal is the constant care of Austin Lawrence and being so it was felt that if HHG focused on three primary guidelines, those of "reconstruction, health of Heathen communities, and a promotion of Heathenry grounded in reality,"[vii] the folk would benefit. This would also offer a foot into Heathenry to new and inquiring Heathens which is not dominated by the internet, but grounded in a physical community where an organic development can occur.

One of the most important aspects of HHG is the giving of rings. It was decided early on by the organizers that it was important to have a significant physical manifestation of the bonds of community which could be gifted by the folk to the folk. In the Elder traditions, it was the responsibility of the tribal leader to confer onto their peers gifts, which in turn strengthened the bonds of fealty. In this same vein, two silver arm rings were commissioned from Jeff Helmes to be given to two worthy members of the community: one to represent a service to the folk, and another to represent a service to the faith. As a portion of the admission price went directly to the purchase of these rings, it made the bond such rings presented real and significant to providers, givers, and receivers. In the following years, those who received rings in the past would become the council from which the rings unto future recipients are conferred, establishing a gift cycle in perpetuity involving all the folk.

Since the first annual Hail and Horn Gathering, which focused on Odin as chief recipient of our sacrifice, there have been four more years. The second year saw the erecting of a Frigg pole alongside Odin, the third a Freyr pole, the fourth a Freya pole, and in this past summer a pole was lifted to Thor. Heimdall and Syn have been selected as the Regin to honour in 2017. Each passing gathering sees at once the cementing of traditions and customs and a degree of change towards some distant ideal of having a place where vast numbers of Heathens can assemble as once did our Ancestors.

Blót to Odin

Oðinn, Woden, Odin, or some expression of the God, has long been a central and important figure in the pantheon of the Pagan Germanic peoples. He is powerful, wise, and wily. In the cosmology, he was involved in creating the worlds and humankind. He spans life and death. Today he is often viewed as an "All Father," a God both beneficent and baneful. As a deity, Odin is exceedingly complex and most definitely of key importance to the majority of Heathens. As creator of the worlds and humankind, it was most appropriate that the first blót at Raven's Knoll be to Him.

The blóts at HHG are very elaborate since they are the focal point for large community gatherings. The large number of people gathering allows for the pooling of resources and efforts to enable us to offer bigger sacrifices to the Gods and to build and maintain a holy place for them.

Provided here is a ritual script describing the first HHG blót. Austin, as the Goði at Raven's Knoll, served as the Goði for this ritual, which was largely written by him. Brynja Eirdis Chleirich and Jade Pichette were supporting ritual officiates (assistant Gythia) for the ritual. HHG blóts have since followed this rough form, omitting elements of the ritual which set the Vé for the first time.

- - - - - - - - - - ~ - - - - - - - - - -

Introduce the Ritual

At the entrance to the path leading to the Vé clearing …

Austin........Welcome, folk to our ceremony. This ritual is a very special one. It will be the first time, to our knowledge, that a permanent sacred place with idols for the worship of the Norse Gods shall be established in Canada. You are here to participate in this event.

Today we open the space with an offering to Odin. Our offering here is part of a blót to the eldest of the Gods; he who formed Ask and Embla; he who engendered the line of the Kings of Mercia and our Crown; he who stands as an ally of the folk.

Today we will be naming many faces of Odin, calling to him that he may know us and we him. Today we will be binding the nine posts of the holy enclosure – the Vé – with rope – a vé-bond – for the first time to make it sacred. Today we will be offering the ingredients of our feast, as the ancient Heathen Rus did on their voyages from the land of the Swedes and Geats into the dangers of the unknown. The bread and leeks, mead and milk and meat, which we offer will be the same we feast upon in his honour.

We will soon proceed into the Vé clearing through the thicket of thorns. At the gate we will pause to make an oath of respect for the holy place. We will then dedicate the Vé with calls to Odin in the Nine Worlds as we carry light around the space to claim it, use the hammer to hallow it, and tie the ropes to bind it. After that we will raise the God-pole to the glory of Odin, after which will make our offerings. Finally, bidding our farewells.

Look deep within your flesh and bones to feel your Ancestors! [*Takes three deep breaths.*] Look within your mind's eye to see the spirits! [*Take three deep breaths.*] Look about you and see the sky above ... the trees around ... and the path before you. [*Walks down the path to lead people into the frith-yard.*]

Procession into the Frithyard

Austin and Brynja lead the group into the clearing, and Jade brings up the back of the line. Austin and Brynja stop in front of the gate and have people stand. Jade comes to the front of the group and stands between the gate posts.

Oath at Gate

Jade............ [*Standing hands to the sky, facing the people.*] You stand at the gate! At the door to the Vé.

Jade............ [*Hands at ease.*] This is a holy place, a home for our Gods in

Midgard. It is a frith-yard, a place of peace and good thoughts. Within this dread enclosure we are in the presence of the Gods. To enter and participate in the ritual, an oath is demanded. If your conscience or abilities will not allow you keep to this oath within the confines of the Vé, please turn back now. Please remove all signs or symbols from your person not honouring the Æsir or Vanir and leave anything that might be considered a weapon behind. Also, please turn off and leave behind all electronic equipment that is not a medical necessity.

All .... *Jade receives oaths from Austin and then from Brynja in turn. All oaths are made on the silver gift arm ring used throughout the event.*

Will you honour only the Æsir, Vanir, their clear allies, and those bound in loyalty to them by blood-oath, within this vé, in both your words and actions?

[After each question the response is "I will"*.]*

Will you carry no weapons into the presence of the Gods?

Will you ensure that no filth of your body touches the ground or any object in this holy place?

Will you keep frith between Gods and folk?

Jade .... *[Auz, then Brynja, enter after this exchange.]* Hail. And … enter the holy grounds.

Jade .... I stand before you as a daughter of the folk; a valkyrie for frith. *[Holding the silver ring in the air.]* I will keep frith between Gods and folk and keep the oath of this frith-yard.

Jade .... *[Austin and Brynja take up positions in front of the hörgr. Jade addresses the rest of the folk.]* You have heard the oath. You stand before your Gods and Ancestors. It is now for each of you to swear on the holy ring of this meeting of folk. To do so binds your doom to this ritual and to the Gods.

Will you keep frith between Gods and folk and keep the oath of this frith-yard?

Individual responses.

Hail. And … enter the holy grounds.

Repeat for everyone. Jade places the ring on the hörgr and returns to stand in the gateway.

Dedication of the Vé

Austin........We now stand in the holy enclosure. We are here to make sacred this place for the first time, to consecrate a vé in which to honour our Gods. Today we raise a God-pole to Odin.

First, we must dedicate our sacred place by drawing a boundary around this garð so that all the Nine Worlds know this is where the Awesome Steed rides between the worlds … where the voices in the Halls of the Ancestors are echoed in Midgarð … where Folk meet the Regin.

Brynja........You see around you nine posts, one for each of the Nine Worlds, from root to branch of the World Tree. Each has already been planted upon a gift offered to the Æsir, Ásynjur and Landvættir. By flame and by hammer, we will honour and bind these offerings to this place in the name of All-Father Odin, the Drighten Wodan.

Brynja........*Auz swings hammer quietly intoning "Thunor weoh" before Brynn; Jade carries lantern with lit candle behind Brynja. Brynja carries the vé-bond rope, starting at the left gate post, working clockwise.*

Oh Gangleri! Traveller in Middle-Earth. Friend of Sigurð. The folk are here before you to set the pale of our sacred Vé, for the glory of the holy Æsir and fortune for the folk. [*Strings and ties vé-bond rope.*] Hail!

Oh Draugadróttinn! Mover of Niflheim. Slayer of Ymir. The folk are here before you to set the pale of our sacred Vé, for the glory of the holy Æsir and fortune for the folk. [*Strings vé-bond rope.*] Hail!

Oh Darraðr! Enemy of Muspellsheim. Father of Víðarr. The folk are here before you to set the pale of our sacred Vé, for the glory of the holy Æsir and fortune for the folk. [*Strings vé-bond rope.*] Hail!

Oh Svipall! Binder of Helheim. Commander of the Völva. The folk are here before you to set the pale of our sacred Vé, for the glory of the holy Æsir and fortune for the folk. [*Strings vé-bond rope.*] Hail!

Oh Hrami! Ring-giver of Svartálfaheim. Prisoner of Reginn Hreiðmarrson. The folk are here before you to set the pale of our sacred Vé, for the glory of the holy Æsir and fortune for the folk. [*Strings vé-bond rope.*] Hail!

Oh Fjörgynn! Plow of Vanaheim. Receiver of Freya. The folk are here before you to set the pale of our sacred Vé, for the glory of the holy Æsir and fortune for the folk. [*Strings vé-bond rope.*] Hail!

Oh Galdraföðr! Howe-dweller in Alfheim. Friend of Frey. The folk are here before you to set the pale of our sacred Vé, for the glory of the holy Æsir and fortune for the folk. [*Strings vé-bond rope.*] Hail!

Oh Bolverk! Foe of Jötunheim. Guest of Vafþrúðnir. The folk are here before you to set the pale of our sacred Vé, for the glory of the holy Æsir and fortune for the folk. [*Strings vé-bond rope.*] Hail!

Oh Alföðr! Lord of Asgard. Lover of Frigg. The folk are here before you to set the pale of our sacred Vé, for the glory of the holy Æsir and fortune for the folk. [*Strings and ties vé-bond rope.*] Hail!

Dedication of the Odin God-Pole

Jade and Brynja prepare the offerings for the dedication of the God-pole, while Austin introduces this part of the ritual.

Austin........ After Hroptatýr formed All-That-Is from the flesh and blood and bones of the Jötunn Ymir, he fashioned the first man and woman out of wood found lying upon the strand. All humanity is tied to all life and to the Gods. It is through the breath of the Galdraföðr, through Ask and Embla, through our Ancestors and the land, that these ties are bound. A gift deserves a gift. Fjölnir recognized the folk in a block of wood, so shall we the

Gods.

Blessings are made with the water drawn from the Sacred Well of Raven's Knoll.

Brynja........ Here are the sacred waters from the Well of Nerthus. Waters flowing from the darkness, from the roots of the World Tree, to the light, under the shining face of Sunna. [*Austin dips tamarack twigs*[viii] *in the offering.*]

Jade removes the cloth covering the God-pole's face.

Austin........ By the pure waters of the well, arise Hangatyr! [*Austin flicks water on the pole and refills.*]   By the wise waters of the well, arise Runatyr! [*Austin flicks water on the pole and refills.*] By the silent waters of the well, arise Blindi! Hail! [*All Hail.*]

Brynja makes ready the honey-water mixed with red ochre.

Brynja........ Here is what wrought the Mead of Poetry. Amber sunlight fettered by bees with the flesh of Jord. Of frith, an oath of spittle; of spittle, a God Kvasir; of Kvasir, earthy wisdom; of wisdom, dwarven greed; of greed, spilled blood; of blood, holy mead; of mead, Ginnarr returns. [*Austin dips tamarack twigs in the offering.*]

Austin........ By Kvasir's blood, arise Woden! [*Austin flicks the potion on the pole and refills.*] By Kvasir's blood, arise Óðr! [*Austin flicks the potion on the pole and refills.*] By Kvasir's blood, arise Ofnir! Hail! [*All Hail.*]

Brynja makes ready an infusion of wormwood and bog myrtle, as well as Midsummer herbs.[ix]

Brynja........ Here is a strong herbed brew. Crafted from plants harvested under the tide of Midsummer for joy and life, and local gruit herbs to make the sorcery of alu. [*Austin dips tamarack twigs in the offering.*]

Austin........ By wort-craft, arise Bileygr! [*Austin flicks the potion on the pole and refills.*] By wort-craft, arise Völsi! [*Austin flicks the potion on the pole and refills.*] By wort-craft, arise Þund! Hail! [*All Hail.*]

Raising of the God-Pole

Jade .... All right, folks. Odin lives. Let's get Him on his feet! Folk who are ready, come on over to help lift Him up ...

Many hands assist with erecting the God-pole; it is centred and the soil tamped down. Everyone again assembles and settles back in front of the hörgr.

Austin .... Hail to Bilygr, the Awestruck Stave! [*All Hail.*] Hail Hávi, the High One! [*All Hail.*] Hail Hoarr, the One-Eyed! [*All Hail.*]

Greetings to Odin

Jade .... Váfuðr returns. Gangleri visits. Let us welcome Him with a song that has been prepared.

Jade introduces and sings the Woden Chant by Michaela Macha (Macha, 2014), getting as many people to sing along as possible.

Wodanaz, Raven-As,
hey-o, Wodanaz !
Wodanaz, Wodanaz,
hey-o-aah !

Hangatyr, Hangatyr,
hey-o, Hangatyr,
Hangatyr, Hangatyr,
hey-o-aah !

Allfather, Allfather,
hey-o, Allfather,
Allfather, Allfather,
hey-o-aah !

Fimbultyr,....
Farmagudh,...
Gangleri,...
Sigfather,...
Hroptatyr,...
Valfather,...
Hrafnass,...
Runatyr,...
Jafnhar,...

Sanngetall,...

Brynja........ Hail!

Offerings from the Folk

Austin........ Oh, Bruni! We are gathered here the folk of the Hail and Horn Gathering. We gather to honour you from many places; from Raven's Knoll, to Douglas, to Huntsville, to Ottawa, to Montreal, to Calgary. Here I stand, I am Austin Pedersen Lawrence, from Raven's Knoll.

Brynja........ I am Patricia Brynn Hultquist, from Ottawa.

Jade............ I am Jade Aurora Pichette, from Ottawa.

Each of the people introduces themselves to Odin, by name and place of origin. Then Austin goes on his knees before the God-pole.

Austin........ Oh, Jormundr! We have brought you gifts. [*Brynja and Jade place the offerings on the hörgr.*] Here we have brought you beef, oats, leeks, onions, milk, ale, bread, butter, cakes, and apples. We have made you this home, this place at Raven's Knoll, and this place in our hearts.

Austin prostrates himself face-down on the ground and rises onto his knees again.

Austin........ Oh, Sigtýr! We have brought you these gifts. We wish that you send us fortune and good harvests in our lives.

Austin prostrates himself face-down on the ground and rises onto his knees again.

Austin........ Oh, Thekkr! We have brought you these gifts. We wish that you join us at húsel and symbel, that we may know the ecstasy of joining folk and Ancestors and Gods.

Austin prostrates himself face-down on the ground and rises onto his knees again.

Brynja........ Ah, Karl. We hope that you are content with your Children of Midgard.

Jade............ Hár, we honour you. Folk, let our offerings be accepted by the High One! Thrice hail ... Hail! Hail! Hail! [*Folk repeat 'Hails' after*

Jade.]

Farewell from the Folk

Austin........ Odin has many faces. Each of us in the Vé is a different pattern in the weave and weft of the Primal Layers. Some of you know Him well, some of you are just getting to know Him.

Brynja and Jade prepare a large horn of ale to toast Odin.

Austin........ In this place, you now have the opportunity for a short personal toast to Odin. If you do not feel moved to speak just take a drink in silence or pass the horn on. We will pour out the remainder of the horn as a drink for Odin at the end of the circle.

Austin steps forward to face Odin, raising the horn. Austin makes a short, extemporaneous toast to Odin, personal with emotion. Then Brynja, then Jade, then the rest of the folk do the same. After each toast everyone "Hails". The horn goes back to Austin for him to pour out on the hörgr.

Austin........ Farewell Langbarðr. [*Austin salutes the God-pole with a raised and open right hand, then pauses and drops his hand.*]

Jade............ This rite is ended! [*Jade stomps on the ground.*]

Procession from the Frith-yard

Brynja........ Let us process from the Vé. [*Leads the folk out of the frith-yard.*]

- - - - - - - - - - ~ - - - - - - - - - -

Other Rites in the Vé

The Raven's Knoll Vé is also used for other Heathen rituals and ceremonies, particularly when the rites involve interacting with the Æsir or require a mythological movement between the Nine Worlds. For instance, parts of Joven Wolf Pearce-Lawrence's manhood ceremony took place within the Vé so that they were witnessed by the Gods, and a number of oracular rites have taken place in the Vé.

People sometimes come to the Vé to finalize the creation of ritual objects or simply to meditate and contemplate situations or the lore. Omens can be read in how offerings are received, wind moves in the leaves of the surrounding trees, or animals move through the space. For instance, when animals quickly consume an offering it can be seen as a good sign. In particular, when an animal associated with a God is seen, an omen might be read more strongly. The day after the Odin blót, Austin returned to the Vé and found that all the food offerings, except the onions,ˣ had been consumed. He startled a pair of large crows from the bush just to the left of the enclosure who rather clumsily flew behind the Odin God-pole off into the sky on the right. (They may have flown rather heavily due to their full bellies.)

Offerings from the year that are not eaten, such as weaving materials, coins, rings and jewelry, horns, rune staves and the like, are collected by Austin and ritually deposited in the Sacred Well at Raven's Knoll at the end of every camping season.

What is important to understand about the Vé is that it is a place where one steps out of the mundane world and enters, concretely so, into that of the sacred. How each person relates to the sacred is a matter of personal theology. However, how a group interacts with the Gods is a careful and meticulous approach outlined by the goði(s) so as to ensure that the efforts of the whole are best presented and accepted by the Gods.

It is by way of this ever-waxing exchange that the people who come to Raven's Knoll come to know the Gods. By entering into a relationship of worth with each other and gifting the Gods, the Vé deepens its place in an evolving sacral landscape, a place where physical and mythical geography can overlap, where the mundane becomes sacred. Such as is demonstrated above, when the folk gather for blót, the Vé offers a centre through which human and God can better communicate and around which our maturing tradition can revolve.

Conclusion

The establishment of the Vé at Raven's Knoll has started to bring about a shift in regional Heathen (and Pagan) religious praxis. Since the inception of this holy stead, the concept of a holy enclosure, totally and utterly separate from the mundane and incorruptible, has caught on among those Heathens who have experienced it. It had been the standard for Pagans to set-up temporary holy spaces for the performance of religious work and to subsequently "bring down" the boundaries separating the sacred and the profane. This was true for many kindreds such as Runatyr Kindred, who once practiced the use of "mobile" vé-bonds to erect a place of worship wherever was most convenient to the folk. Now, Runatyr Kindred has erected a permanent Vé in a similar fashion as that at Raven's Knoll, as a fixed cult centre, inspired by the Raven's Knoll Vé. The folk of Thornhaven have also erected a Vé dedicated to the worship of their holy powers on private land. It seems when something is viewed as good for the folk, it inspires many people.

Raven's Knoll is a special place for all those who visit and help it grow. As such the input of the folk means a lot to the stewards of the land as well as the organizers of the many festivals. At the Hail and Horn Gathering, the folk who attend participate in a very important feedback and decision making forum known as the *Redemoot*. This Redemoot is a gathering of the folk to give wise counsel so as to better the decision-making of organizers and volunteers in the preparation of the next year's gathering. On the final day, the attendees deliberate, exchange ideas, and vote on the next year's theme, specifically which God(dess) is to be worshiped next. Since 2012, the divinities most favoured by the folk have been Odin, Frigg, Freyr, Freya, and Thor. After years of discussion of putting up two smaller poles to form a threshold in the Vé, depicting a God and Goddess of the folk with influence over liminal spaces and oaths, 2017 will finally see Heimdall and Syn be the focus of the folk's veneration. This means that the form that the blót will take, what workshops will be held, and what foods to feast upon are to be based upon known lore of the two deities' mythos.

There are many ideas brewing among the folk of Raven's Knoll and the direction in which they would like to see the sacred character of the land evolve. For starters, there are many more Gods and Goddesses to be added to the Vé, but whom and how many are still to be determined by the folk in coming years. There is also talk of putting up God-poles to honour Tyr, Ullr, and Skaði, amongst others. A goodly number of the folk wished to see a God-pole to the One-With-Sewn-Maw, Loki, go up outside the Vé. It is recognized that not everyone agrees with venerating the Jötunn, but that such practice is important to many folk. Thus, at the first steps of the Shrine Path, one the main paths leading to the Vé, there is a pole with his image off to the side and an enclosure for more representations of his allies and kin. For many wishing to go to the Vé of the Æsir, it seems only appropriate to pay a short visit to Laufey's Son before beginning the journey.

Another important goal to the folk is the eventual building of a hof or a meadhall. This would help with húsel and symbel as it would offer a very appropriate venue for both. Exactly when and how such a building or buildings will go up are left up to those who pine to see such a project through. Such a construct would bring and bind the people together as in ancient days.

To be in the Raven's Knoll frith-yard is to feel the ancient wisdom, to connect with the Gods and the Ancestors. All folk, no matter background or belief, who hold a sincere wish to know the Old Gods of the North and are respectful of tradition, are invited and welcome to become part of the community that uses this sacred space.

Book Hoard

Adam of Bremen. *History of the Archbishops of Hamburg-Bremen.* trans. Francis J. Tschan. New York: Columbia University Press, 2002.

Anonymous. *Eyrbyggja Saga.* trans. Hermann Pálsson and Paul Edwards. London: Penguin Books, 1972, 1989.

Bycok, Jesse. *Viking Age Iceland.* London: Penguin Books, 2001.

Ellis-Davidson, Hilda R. *Myths and Symbols in Pagan Europe: Early Scandinavian and Celtic Religions.* Syracuse: Syracuse University Press, 1988.

Gunnel, Terry. "Hof, Halls, Goðar and Dwarves: An Examination of the Ritual Space in the Pagan Icelandic Hall," *Cosmons* 17:1 (June 2001), 3-36.

Lucas, Gavin. *Hofstaðir: Excavations of a Viking Age Feasting Hall in North-Eastern Iceland.* Reykyavík: Institute of Archeology Monograph Series, 1, 2009.

Macha, Michaela. *Odin's Gift: Norse Mythology and Asatru Music and Poetry.* Accessed November 14, 2014 from http://www.odins-gift.com/index.html.

Pollington, Stephen. *The Mead-hall: Feasting in Anglo-Saxon England.* Norfolk: Anglo-Saxon Books, 2003.

Ravencast Podcast. Episode 46: *"Groves and Sacred Spaces".* Accessed November 14, 2014 from http://www.podcasts.com/ravencast_-_the_asatru_podcast/episode/episode_46_-_groves_and_sacred_spaces.

Raven Kindred North. *Raven Kindred North.* Accessed November 14, 2014 from http://www.ravennorth.org/.

Simek, Rudolk. *Dictionary of Northern Mythology.* Stuttgart: Alfred Kröner Verlag, 1993.

Simpson, Jacqueline. *Everyday Life in the Viking Age.* New York: Dorset, 1967.

Sturluson, Snorri. *The Prose Edda.* trans. Jesse L. Byock. London: Penguin Classics, 2005.

Tacitus. *Germania*. trans. H. Mattingly, trans. revised S.A. Handford. London: Penguin Classics, 1948, 1970.

Viking Answer Lady. *Risala: Ibn Fadlan's Account of the Rus*. Accessed November 11, 2014 from http://www.vikinganswerlady.com/ibn_fdln.shtml.

Viking Answer Lady. *Sacred Space in Viking Law and Religion*. Accessed November 11, 2014 from http://www.vikinganswerlady.com/sacspace.shtml.

Venerable Bede. *Bede's Ecclesiastical History of the English People*. ed. Bertram Colgrave and R.A.B.Mynors. Oxford: Clarendon, 1969.

Wikipedia. *Vé (shrine)*. Accessed November 11, 2014 from http://en.wikipedia.org/wiki/V%C3%A9_(shrine).

Endnotes:

i. *Miðgarð*, or Midgard, which translates as "Middle-Earth" is one of the many worlds in Heathen cosmology. It corresponds with the Earth, the world of ordinary human experience.

ii. Dinars and dirhems were a silver-based currency of a number of Muslim empires.

iii. Rede "counsel, advice, (archaic)" from Old English *ræd* "advice, counsel."

iv. Austin Lawrence in correspondence.

v. Onetime annual meeting of members of the Rúnatýr Kindred and their Innangard. Executive, judicial and legislative in nature.

vi. Meaning, for the organizers, that these two aspects are primal and shared motifs to which most modern Heathens could relate.

vii. Austin Lawrence, personal communication with Erik Lacharity.

viii. At Raven's Knoll, the hlaut-tines, the asperging twigs used for the ritual sprinkling of liquids, are usually ritually cut from one of the tamarack trees. Usually, a tree associated with Yggdrasil such as ash is used. However, Raven's Knoll is not in the right climatic location to grow ash. As a result, the North American version of the larch, known in parts of Norway as the "needle ash," is used instead. It is a tricky tree that appears to court death, yet survives; it grows in boggy soil and its green needles turn golden each autumn making what appeared to be an evergreen into a bare skeleton.

ix. A significant number of Canadian Heathens have French-Canadian ancestry, including one of the co-founders of the Hail and Horn

Gathering, Erik Lacharity. Many with Franco-Canadian heritage trace their roots to Normandy, the part of modern France settled by Vikings from what is now Denmark. Heathen religious practices may have survived in many folk beliefs, including a popular one being revived amongst Franco-Canadian Heathens, which is the collection of particular herbs at Midsummer for the use in charms and rituals throughout the year.

x. It turns out almost nothing living at the Knoll likes to eat anything from the onion family. The offerings stick around for months until they sprout!

Austin Lawrence is known in the Pagan community as "Auz." He is one of the Stewards of Raven's Knoll and a co-organizer of the Kaleidoscope Gathering. Auz has a Master's degree in Anthropology and is a Heathen who is an oathed Goði that serves as the Keeper of the Raven's Knoll Vé. Auz is also a former Stag King of the Kaleidoscope Gathering. He lives in Ottawa with his wife Maryanne Pearce, his two adult children Kadri Rainne and Joven Wolf, and a menagerie of family pets.

Erik Lacharity currently resides just outside of Ottawa, Ontario, Canada with his lovely, and ever supportive, wife Chantal and their two girls, Scarlet and Rosabel. He grew up in the small sleepy hamlet of Danford Lake in rural Québec and enjoys all the benefits and hard lessons which come from being a country boy. In 2006, after a long search in matters of religion, he settled upon Heathenry and two years later co-founded Rúnatýr Kindred. He also co-founded the Hail and Horn Gathering with Austin Lawrence in 2011, the same year his pursuits in Frankish Reconstructionism led him to found *Thia Frankisk Aldsido* (The Old Frankish Custom). He also loves French-Canadian folk magic and revitalizing the ancient Bear Cult.

HOW I FOUND THE KNOLL

by Gypsy Birch

I came to Raven's Knoll for the first time in 2011. At first glance, it might seem to be a random bit of luck that led me to the land, but when I looked back at the course of my life it became apparent that there were many different events that put me on my path to the Knoll.

In the spring of 2011, I attended the Beltane/Maypole Work Weekend. It was the first Pagan event I had ever attended, and I wasn't sure how I was going to fit in. Only a few hours into the weekend, I knew that this was the right place for me, that this was the land that I was meant to be on. That first night, as I lay in bed after the Walpurgisnacht ritual that was held with a small group around a campfire, I texted a friend and told her that I had "found my people".

Fitting in socially had always been a difficult task for me. I struggled with conversation, continuously second-guessing and regretting the ways in which I was able to present myself. As a child, I always felt different from my friends and family in a way that I could never define or explain. I had intense dreams and nightmares that I often kept to myself, not having the words or understanding to properly convey the images that I saw. I was a nervous and often-frightened child, but kept those parts of myself concealed as much as possible. Overnight visits with friends often had to be cut short because I couldn't sleep away from home. The comfort of my own bed was something that was incredibly important.

Over time, my ability to spend nights away from home became acceptable enough that my parents decided to send me to a summer camp. Admittedly, this was a bit of a concern for me, but I was reaching an age when the prospect of learning about things like archery and canoeing was substantial enough to outweigh the fears. So, the decision made, I was sent to a non-denominational Christian camp that focused on horsemanship, and it was no secret that I greatly enjoyed my week away from home. I enjoyed it so much, in fact, that I returned the next year. The year after that, I went for a two-week duration. After five years of being a camper and having built up to three-week stays, I moved into the training process of learning how to be a camp counselor, and ended up working at the camp for the next four years. I had moved from a frightened child to being an archery instructor, a snorkeling trainer, a leader of biking expeditions, an assistant in the horse corral, and a respected fisherman. I learned the woods and the waterways of the camp's land as though they were my own.

I became close with the family that ran the camp. Some of the sons were very near to my age, and lasting friendships were formed. The shenanigans and pranks we played were not just limited to the other camp staff, but I will openly admit that there were those of us at the camp who found great amusement in hopping the fence and strolling casually through the campground next door. We did not feel as though we were doing wrong. Folks from that neighbouring campground often had loud electronic music and concerts that went well into the early hours of the morning, frustrating and annoying us at the kids' camp. It was also not unusual to find refuse tossed carelessly over the fence onto the kids camp's property. Still, we tried not to harass or bother the campground, and usually just strolled through a quiet roadway under cover of darkness, eventually retreating through a field of knee-high pine saplings and hopping back over the fence.

As I aged, however, my college-bound future required me to find more gainful employment than being a camp counselor, and with a heavy heart, I spent my last summer before college working retail.

After graduation, I bounced from job to job for years, struggling to find comfort in the occupations I found. If I was with an employer for a year, it was a rarity, for I always felt compelled to move on and to find something more meaningful.

When I turned twenty-five, my father passed away. His death struck me very hard, as there had been no warning signs of ill health. It happened a week before I was set to head back to college in search of a new career path, and I did my best to move forward with life. I knew that despite my positive intent, I was mentally in a dark place, and needed something to brighten the world I was living in. With that as my focus, I returned to the camp for the summer of my college break, as well as for the summer after graduation.

Returning to the camp had two consecutive effects. First, I realized that sometimes it is better to leave good memories where they are, lest you try to reconstruct them and learn that you can never truly relive that which has gone by. Second, I learned that new memories can be made that may outshine the old, and trying to live in the past is an unnecessary struggle. Making new friends does not mean leaving the old friends behind, it means growing and enjoying the world as it is, not as it was.

Something else happened during my time at the camp, but it was not specific to me. At first it was spoken of only in hushed whispers, delivered as a rumoured gossip that was not meant to be spoken of openly. However, the truth was not to be concealed for long, and it became public knowledge that the land next to the kids camp, which had long-since closed as a campground, had been purchased by "witches." This naturally created much unfounded speculation and fear-mongering, but I found myself quite intrigued.

Witches? What exactly did that mean? Who were these people? Were they legitimate practitioners of a spiritual path that I knew of only from what I had seen in film? Was the whole thing some great misunderstanding? Whatever the answer, I could not leave it alone.

I drove past the entrance to the newly-purchased land whenever I left the kids camp, and upon a small hill I saw a sign that read "Raven's Knoll." This was enough of a start for me, and I began to search for answers. The internet was immediately helpful, and I found myself staring at contact information for the owners of the land. I was very hesitant at first, wondering how they would react to a stranger reaching out with questions.

The struggle was short lived. I sent an e-mail to Austin Lawrence, one of the owners, and I asked what sort of events happened on the land, and what I could expect if I attended. At the time, I made no mention of my connection to the kids camp. Austin was forthcoming with his answers, but definitely leaned towards a "come on out and see for yourself" mentality. Unfortunately my first contact with him had been after Raven's Knoll summer season was already over, and so I prepared myself to attend the next year's first spring event, the Beltane and Maypole Work Weekend.

I arrived with my little tent trailer, and my first on-site contact was with Brendan Roche, the resident caretaker of the land, and Kevin McLaughlin, a coworker of his. I set up my trailer in what I later learned was the festival vendor area known as Diagon Alley (not in use that weekend, fortunately), and within minutes of completion I was able to start assisting in clearing brush and trees that had come down over the winter.

The attendance that weekend was not vast. I met new people whose faces would become very familiar to me over the next few years, even though I did not realize it at the time: MA (the other landowner), Rya, Jade, Nic, Melody, Grey, and more.

That night in my trailer, when I texted that I had "found my people," it was even more true than I realized at the time. These were people that I would come to fest with, work with, share good times, and share sad times.

For those first few weeks, I kept quiet about how I had found the land, casually explaining that I often drove through the area and had been curious about the meaning of the Raven's Knoll sign. This explanation seemed satisfactory enough to all. I wanted to learn as much as I could without fear that I was "with the neighbours." It wasn't until that year's Midgard Festival that I decided to explain how I had come to Raven's Knoll.

I signed myself up for the Bardic Competition, and stood in front of a crowd to tell my tale. I saw more than one open-mouthed expression of surprise at this revelation of how I had come to the community. It is a fair assumption to make that they did not expect someone to have come over from the camp next door. There was much in the way of positive reactions to my story. I got a few "formal" welcomes to the community, but truly, they were done in such a way that I really felt like they were saying "welcome home."

As I write this, it has been almost four seasons since I found my way to the Knoll. I have since become a member of Kaleidoscope Gathering's staff, an organizer of multiple Raven's Knoll events, and a regular work weekend attendee. I have had my hand on all the Asatru God-poles that have gone into the ground. I teach many of the same things at the Knoll that I did at the kids' camp.

It is still strange to me, and perhaps always will be, to think that I once strolled down a road now known as Bogside before the land was called Raven's Knoll. I strode through a field of saplings that now tower over me, and in which I assist rituals. I know the portion of river that borders the Knoll more than I know the river down the road from where I lived for thirty-three years.

Pondering the events of my life, I realize that they may not be dramatic or spectacular. They may even seem bland and uninteresting. But I do know this: had it not been for the way my life has unfolded, and the directions I was pushed, I would not have found Raven's Knoll. I now understand that sometimes, darkness exists in our lives because without it we would not go searching for the right light.

Gypsy Birch is a member of Raven's Knoll staff, performing such duties as security and maintenance, as well as assists in organization for multiple events. He is also part of the Flying Monkey security team for the Kaleidoscope Gathering. While he has no defined personal practice pertaining to a particular spiritual path, Gypsy assists followers of many different faiths to ensure that their event or ritual meets the logistical needs of the organizers and attendees.

THE WITCHES' SABBAT,
HORNED LORD RITE

by Ryan "Anthos" Sauvé

An account of a devotional weekend for the Horned Lord, in all His forms, which was the first Witches' Sabbat at Raven's Knoll event.

As the wheels rolled down the pavement, I was treated to a lazy ride with two fellow witches, from home to what would hopefully be Elsewhere. One napped, one drove, and I picked their brains for philosophical and magical silver threads that I could weave into my witchy web.

We arrived in the daylight with little time to spare. The clang of a bell called the witches together around the camp's Hearth fire, and everything was quickly underway.

We began by processing through the terrain, visiting the sacred sites and leaving offerings. Libations were poured, fruits and gifts laid out on the ground, and voices cried out in praise and greeting:

"HAIL THE RIVER!"

"HAIL THE MOUNDS!"

"HAIL THE STONES! THE TREES! THE FIRES!"

"HAIL THE SPIRITS, THE CREATURES, THE ANCESTORS, AND THE KEEPERS OF THIS PLACE!"

All the spirits were thanked and honoured as we witches placed offerings in their homesteads. Even those of us without physical gifts offered a bowed head, a warm nod, or an open space amongst our group for the weekend.

At each sacred place where we laid our offerings, a gift was found in kind; some witches' tool that cunning folk have built their crafts upon, and a secret held in each one that said to us "I am useful. I am part of a whole. I am more than a tool. By your hands I will be so much more. By my own power I am so much more".

Following the processional, we regrouped briefly as a plan was laid. Then, dinner and the chance to mingle and enjoy our communal fire.

As darkness fell, and as bellies were filled, we gathered around the Hearth fire in the centre of our camp. Introductions were made in little groups, and drinks were shared. Soon we took to telling stories. The brave and bardic told classic stories, while some others traipsed round the circle, singing songs. Standing still, poems were shared. Our leaders for the weekend, Angela and Juniper, each taking a turn. Angela painted us verbal pictures of the Yukon, and Juniper told us a story of a naive young witch and her life changing folly, while her trusted canine followed her every step and turn around the flames.

Stories kept on and went, and as the night wore on some stayed, cradling our bodies closer to the fire, while others gave in and left to sleep. Conversations evolved, and helpful tips exchanged; what to do with an odorous skull, or how to find a good book. Witchy and common subjects alike, as more silver threads were added to my web.

A witch, to some, is a nocturnal creature, so it was no surprise when sleeping in was permitted the next day. A late start meant a late night to come, and so we gathered around the Hearth fire once more in the midday sun to really begin our weekend. Introductions were made, and what a motley crew we were: BritTrad Wiccans, New Agers, ecstatic witches, theistic Pagans, Heathens, parents, children, young, old, new, and adepts. All there to experience something new. Something wild, and maybe something a bit darker than we'd allow ourselves any other time.

We were also introduced to our herb for the weekend, *Artemisia absinthium*. Wormwood. A classic witching herb found in Absinth, known for its sensual effects and its ability to push a person on and on.

We sat, following the shade, and discussed…everything. Wormwood. Witchcraft. Ecstasy. And, of course, the Gods. Because as we sat, the gifts given to us during our opening procession were laid out and we began to piece them slowly together: A loose robe. A horned stag skull. A strong and impressive stang. Linseed oil. Sewing tools. Everything we needed to create a stunning and terrifying effigy of the Horned Lord. Each of us was able to contribute: embroidery, or a woven rope, or a beaded string, or a braided garland of feathers and flowers. A powerful blend of classic cunningfolk herbs and ingredients were mixed together to form a red paste which we used to bless the skull, and give Him flesh once more.

I created kernips for myself at the Horned God altar, before my portrait of Dionysus Dikerôtês (Dionysus, the Two-Horned) to whom I am devoted, and cleansed myself of miasma before our ritual.

After all the gift-pieces were assembled on that strong and beautiful stang, and I was lucky enough to be chosen to carry it; to carry the Horned Lord, high above my head at the front of our processional to the ritual space. I was the very first stang-bearer at the very first Witches' Sabbat!

We processed from our Hearth fire to the Witches' Circle: a spiraling path through the woods, ending in our open ritual space. Drums beating heavily and somberly, and a clanging tambourine tossing clattering noises from the back, we marched to the Witches' Circle.

"HAIL THE HORNED LORD!"

"HAIL THE SPIRITS!"

"HAIL!"

"HAIL!"

When we arrived we were offered our choice of wormwood: a flying ointment, a powerful and bitter tincture, or a sachet of herbs to carry around with us. Each made their choice, considering their tolerances, experience, and how they wished to approach the sacred herb, and how that would affect this ecstatic ritual celebration of the Horned Lord. One by one we slipped onto the spiral path, having been warned "This path is far longer than you anticipate. Keep walking. Keep silent. Keep going."

This may have been truer for me than anyone.

As the stang-bearer, I entered last, and could not see the path before me. The Horned Lord's robe hung before my face like a veil, and I simply walked forward in silence, eyes down and followed the sound of drumming and chanting as the sun set, safely guided by Juniper and Angela. The spiral went on and on. I could see the shapes of humans beside me, deeper into the path, but I could not tell each from another. I could hear their song, and the drums they chanted over, but every time I felt that I was closing in on them, the path stretched on and on ahead of me.

I finally arrived, and cries flew up into the darkening sky;

"HE HAS COME!"

"HE HAS ARRIVED!"

"THE HORNED LORD! HAIL!"

"PRAISE!"

"BEHOLD!"

The ritual was started; a hedge raised, and bottles and bottles of offerings laid out before the Horned God's feet. Gifts and tokens of appreciation placed in the sand, which had turned red and fragrant with wine and other libations.

And then the dancing.

Sometimes powerful experiences should be kept secret. This may be one of those times. But I can tell you that it was as if I had been caught in a river, dragging me forward, even when my mind knew I could have stopped. I didn't want to, though. I wanted to continue. Wormwood pushed me on. The Horned Lord pushed. Dionysus pushed me, as I swung my hair about and threw my head back, exposing my throat to the moon. Dancing and dancing, spinning and spinning. Round and round and round and thrumming and shaking and drumming and rattling and on and on and on…

"HAIL THE HORNED LORD!"

"HAIL OLD HORNY!"

"HAIL! PAN! DIONYSUS! CERNUNNOS! MASTER!"

"HAIL BAPHOMET, LIGHT BRINGER!"

"HAIL! HAIL! HAIL!"

Until we nearly all fell and the world was cold beneath our pulsing bodies.

Everything slowed.

Bread and drink were shared, and thanks given.

The spiral unwound as we walked out of the Witches' Circle.

We headily returned to our camp and Hearth fire, our home base and community centre for the weekend to discuss what happened, but also to just coast on the body buzz of wormwood, ritual, ecstasy and shared experience. More discussions were held: family, the Internet, what "those young'ns" (of which I am one) are up to, knowing the Gods, and making it work.

All weekend the conversation was fluid and open, despite the many backgrounds and paths represented amongst us. We shared a communal stone soup, and were treated with bannock bread by Angela. We joked, and shared more tricks or stories, and learned.

The weekend ended with a final procession, more offerings laid out and more shouts to the sky in honour of the Spirits and sacred places that had housed us for the weekend, enriching our experiences. Then, a discussion of the coming year.

Wheels rolling down the pavement again, a napping witch in the back seat and two chatty ones up front, more threads weaving into my web, more tangles and snares. Some old ones coming undone. The Witches' Sabbat behind us and home ahead, the experiences still flush in our faces.

Honour to the Horned God, and honour to the Knoll. Honour to the witches, and those tools that we use: the needle and thread, wormwood, mushrooms, bones, water, books, bells, and drums!

Ryan (Anthos) is a Dionysian devotee, out-of-practice dancer, and occasional blogger. A witch and Pagan since he was 12, he writes about witchcraft, religion, spirituality, art, and how they all intersect with his queer identity. You can find more of his writing at achangingaltar.wordpress.com, or more frequently you can see what he's been up to on achangingaltar.tumblr.com.

THE JOURNEY OF THESEUS

by Melissa Gold, with Spyros Parashis,
Stephanie Gray and Karen Wehrstein

All things begin with the word, the logos, the mythos. We speak the ancient words, words that first spoke of the hero Theseus and his journey to rescue the youths of Athens from certain death as victims of the Minotaur and many other wonderful deeds. We thus speak of the paths of all heroes.

The words we use are sacred. We speak to the ancient Gods of Greece. The words are inspired by the Muses through playwrights and poets and by the Goddess Athena. We speak these words to you in the common tongue of today.

Hear our words and take part on our pilgrimage as we trace the steps of Theseus and bring honor to our ancestors and the founders of civilization.

This ritual was presented as the main ritual at the Kaleidoscope Gathering 2013 where the theme was "Heroes". It is slightly changed from how it was conducted because all Greek language has been changed to English.

- - - - - - - - - - Ω - - - - - - - - - -

We begin with a procession to the sanctified ground. We march in solemn quietness, carrying our implements with us. At the heart of this space is the sacred hearth and altar; at the perimeter are all those who journey and participate with us. At the edge of the ritual space, we pause to wash our hands, pouring water from a vessel, preparing ourselves for sacred tasks and separating us from all thoughts of mundane and vulgar works. Then we enter, circle around and gather around the altar.

ALPHA: Sanctification of the Precinct

[We use the abbreviation IER for the ritual leader. This comes from the Greek word "iereus", one who conducts sacred ritual.]

IER: As we have prepared ourselves beforehand for this undertaking, now we prepare a place for positive divine energy to appear and mystery to occur. We especially remind all participants that, during these sacred proceedings, we must guard what we say, as we can affect the outcome for now and all time, for ourselves and our community, if we speak in a non-propitious fashion.

The IER goes to the altar and dips a branch of myrtle into the bowl of pure water and sprinkles the altar and images and any offerings on the altar, and then circles the precinct clockwise, sprinkling the boundary and participants along the boundary, while repeating the following sacred saying, until the circuit is complete:

IER: O Gods// turn away evils!
ALL: O Gods// turn away evils!

From Euripides, Phoinissai, lines 586f

When the IER finishes, they set the bowl away from the altar, as the bowl is now ritually impure.

IER: Welcome to our celebration to honor the Heroes and Theseus. It is allowed that all may take part.

IER: Let no one speak an ill-omened word!
ALL: Let no one speak an ill-omened word!

Aristophanes, Thesmophoriazusai, lines 295ff

IER: We think clean thoughts, and we speak words of good omen.
ALL: We think clean thoughts, and we speak words of good omen.

Based on what questioners were told at Delphoi

BETA: Libation to Apollo and Athena

[Apollo and Athena are the gods who guided the steps of Theseus.]

IER: We will now honour the God Apollo and the Goddess Athena, for Athena is the patron god of the paternal city of Theseus and Apollo is the God of Delphi, whose oracles from Delphi led to the birth and leadership of Theseus.

The IERs light the fire and then the incense in the incense stand and throw some incense onto the fire.

IER (*holding libation bowl containing wine toward heaven*):
I will remember and not be unmindful of Apollo who shoots from afar.
As he goes through the house of Zeus, the Gods tremble before him
and all spring up from their seats when he draws near,
as he bends his bright bow.

from *Homeric Hymn III*, to Delian Apollo, lines 1-4

IER:
How then shall I sing of you–though in all ways you are a worthy theme for song?
Shall I sing of how, at the first, you went about the earth seeking a place of oracle for men, O far-shooting Apollo?

IER pours libation onto ground.

from *Homeric Hymn IV*, to Pythian Apollo, lines 207 & 214-215

IER:
As once you taught us:
Stand side by side around the altar and pray…

from *Homeric Hymn IV*, to Pythian Apollo, lines 493 and 500

Hail Healer!

All: Hail Healer! (*7 times*)
IER: To Apollo!
IERs put more incense on the incense stand and in the fire.

IER (*holding libation bowl refilled with wine toward heaven*):
Of Pallas Athena, guardian of the city, I begin to sing.
Awesome is she, and with Ares she loves deeds of war,
The sack of cities and the shouting and the battle.
It is she who saves the people as they go out to war and come back.
Hail, Goddess, and give us good fortune with happiness!

from *Homeric hymn XI*, to Athena

IER:
O warlike Pallas, only child born from great Zeus,
Blessed Goddess, strong of spirit, who raises the din of war
You are ineffable yet it is worthy to tell of you …

46

Female and male by nature, mother of wars,
Ever-changing, ferocious, source of divine influence, worthy of respect …
Hear me, O Goddess, when I pray to you,
Give wealth, bring peace, abundant health
And wealth until my last hours, you who are virgin mother of all arts,
O, much implored, blue-eyed Queen.

from Orphic Hymn 32, to Athena

IER: To Athena!

IER pours libation onto ground.

GAMMA: Retelling the Deeds of Theseus

IER: Hear, ye people! Hear, ye people!

from Plutarch, Lives: Theseus, 13:3

Hear of the hero Theseus, founder of the great city of Athens, who was descended from the noble line of King Erechtheus of Attica, through his father, King Aegeus, and from the royal line of Pelops, from his mother, Aethra, and said to be the son of Poseidon until he reached manhood and claimed his birthright. At that time, he lifted the mighty boulder to claim the token sword and sandals left by his true father and journeyed to join him in Athens.

He shunned the safe voyage by sea and chose instead the difficult journey by land inhabited by robbers and dangerous men. He declared: "I am a match for the violent! The good I spare!"

And Theseus admired the valor of Heracles, his cousin, who once purged the land of the wicked. And Theseus desired to emulate Herakles by destroying criminals and highwaymen, whomsoever had escaped destruction by the great hero.

from Plutarch, Lives: Theseus

IER: Let us pour a libation to Heracles!

IER (*holding libation bowl filled with wine toward heaven*) :
Hear, powerful Heracles, untamed and strong,
To whom vast hands and mighty works belong…
To thee mankind as their deliverer pray,
Whose arm can chase the savage tribes away…
From east to west endured with strength divine,
Twelve glorious labors to absolve is thine;

47

Supremely skilled, thou reignest in heaven's abodes,
Thyself a God amidst the immortal Gods.
With arms unshaken, infinite, divine,
Come, blessed power, and to our rites incline…

from *Orphic Hymn 12* to Heracles

IERs pour libation to Herakles onto ground.

IER: And going out across the land, Theseus destroyed the miscreants of
his day:
> Periphetes, the club-bearer, and took his club (*assistant to IER brings in
> a club*);
> Sinis the Pine-bender (*an assistant to IER brings in a large pine branch*);
> And the Krommyonian Sow, a monstrous beast (*an assistant to IER
> brings in a sword*).

from Plutarch, *Lives: Theseus*

IER: We will now hold sacred games to commemorate the labors of
Theseus! Games have always been part of religious practice in the Hellenic
world.

*The "game" is played as follows: The assistants who brought in the tokens (the club, the
pine branch and a plastic sword), hand them out to three people standing in the circle.
Ideally, the tokens are given to people a third of the way around the circle from each other.
The people now holding the tokens are "captains" of the tokens. When the IER says
"go!", the captains hand the token to the person next to them who passes the token to the
next person in turn and thus the tokens are passed around the circle; two proceed to the
right and one to the left. The captain follows his or her token around the circle. Each
person standing in the circle must touch each token once and pass it on. They must not
drop the tokens or throw them. If they drop them, they must pick them up and wait until
the IERs give them permission to continue; there is a time penalty. The captains want
their token to be the first to return to its starting place, so they urge the participants to
hurry. At some point, two tokens will arrive at the same person at the same time. This
adds to the complexity of the task and the captains may contend with the person holding
the tokens to pass theirs along first. The captain of the token that arrives back to the
start first (to the last person next to their original spot) wins an athletic crown (a wreath
of plants and flowers). The winner's crown and ribbons for the other two captains are
awarded before the ritual continues.*

Theseus goes to Crete

IER: And when Theseus came finally to Athens, to his father King Aegeus,
he presented himself with his tokens.

An assistant acting as Theseus enters and walks around the circle displaying sandals and sword.

IER: But his greatest feat of bravery was going to Crete to kill the Minotaur, a monster that was both man and bull!

According to legend, a Cretan man had been killed treacherously within the confines of Attica, and not only did King Minos wage war against the inhabitants of the country but Heaven also laid it waste with drought and pestilence. The God Apollo commanded the Athenians that, if they appeased Minos, the wrath of Heaven would abate and there would be an end to their misery. The agreement was that they would send a tribute of seven youths and seven maidens once every nine years. It was believed that these young people were destroyed by the Minotaur in the labyrinth of Knossos. It was a grave thing to draw the lot to go to Crete as part of the tribute. On the third occasion of the lots, Theseus was chosen.

from Plutarch, Lives: Theseus

IER: As theatre was also an ancient religious ritual, we will now enact the story of Theseus with those of you who have come here today. We need seven maidens and six young warriors who would like to take part.

The IERs select 13 of the volunteers: six youths, seven maidens (they can be any age), and bring them into the circle; Theseus steps in as the seventh youth and the IER continues.

IER: As we see, Theseus chose to be one of the fourteen! The legend was that, if the Minotaur were killed, the tribute would cease. Theseus said: "It is not fitting for a man with ways like mine to run from danger. I've done honourable deeds; this is the conduct I have chosen toward the Greeks: To be the man who punishes the evil doer".

from Euripides, Suppliant Women, lines 336-339

So, they set out and when Theseus reached Knossos, it is said that he got from Ariadne the yarn that allowed him to make his way through the intricacies of the Labyrinth.

The assistant acting as Theseus arranges the youths around the fire, each holding onto the string, to form a circle of the string, facing outward from the fire.

Youths (*while moving around the circle clockwise*):
O Athena! Save us from the Minotaur!

49

After a minute or two, another assistant acting as the Minotaur runs in, making loud noises and threatening the participants and youths. Theseus drops the yarn, picks up the sword, silences the Minotaur and recruits the youth to chase the Minotaur away.
The chase is played in this way: the Minotaur gets a light head start, then the maidens and youths chase after him. They MUST follow the same course around the circle or around trees, rocks, etc., that the Minotaur follows; no short cuts! The object is to capture the "tail" of the Minotaur (a red kerchief tucked into a belt). Once the "tail" is captured, Theseus arrives and symbolically "slays" the Minotaur. The youth or maiden who captured the tail of the Minotaur is awarded a crown by the IERs in the center of the circle. Ribbons of courage may be awarded to the others. Then the ritual continues.

IER: Theseus killed the Minotaur and returned to Athens with the youths and maidens. In honor of the great deeds of Theseus on Crete, let us now do the labyrinth dance that Theseus learned on his voyage home.

All dance the labyrinth dance, with drummers providing a rhythm. The "dance" may use any kind of step as people in the circle are led by one or more IERs in a twisting complex pathway. Ideally, it spirals in and out and other variations are good. This could go on for a while, as participants wish. It is most important that, during the dance, participants maintain ritual "silence", which means that any word they utter is propitious, kind and considerate, as what is said during a sacred dance is considered a request of the Gods. When the IERs slowly silence the drums, all return to the circle and resume silence. The assistant dressed as the young Theseus departs and changes. An older assistant dressed as Theseus enters the ritual area.

Man of Peace

IER: As a King, Theseus was a man of peace! He unified Attica. He is the founder of the city of Athens. And it is he who instituted democracy. He was a man of "reverence and righteousness, justice and humanity".

based on Plutarch, Lives, Theseus, XXV.1

IER: Hear the words of Theseus:
"…But where the laws are written down both weak and strong,
Both rich and poor, have equal power and equal right…
The small can beat the great with justice on his side…"

Euripides, Suppliant Women, lines 432-433, 436

IER: "This is the kind of general that a city should choose,
One brave in danger, one who hates a violent folk
Who, faring well, still seeks to climb the highest rungs
Of ladders to lose the happiness they might enjoy".

Euripides, Suppliant Women, lines 721-724

IERs:
Come hither all people
The hero proclaimed
Uniting the people
He gathered us in
And gave up his crown
To strengthen the law.

based on Plutarch, *Lives, Theseus*, XXV.1

The Peace Treaty

IER acting as an older Theseus enters and proceed to centre of ritual circle. The King of the land stands in the circle with other participants.

Theseus:
All of us know which is the better and how much
More good peace gives to mortal souls than bloody war.
Peace, the first and best beloved by all the Muses...loves to have good children
Loves to have wealth...we evil fools discard them both whenever we choose war, enslaving men and cities.

Eurpides, *Suppliant Women*, lines 486-491

The wise men then should love their children first of all,
Next those who bore them, next their country, if they wish
To make it great, not break it...

Euripides, *Suppliant Women*, lines 504-8

Enter IER dressed as Athena to the sound of tambourines which stop so that she can speak.

The IER who undertakes this role must wash and meditate before and after undertaking this role, as the energy of the Goddess is invoked inside a human being.

IER, acting as Athena:
Theseus!
Listen to the words of the Goddess Athena! Listen well to my words!
Listen to what you must do for the benefit of your community.

Demand an oath which must be sworn by the king of this place. The king has the authority to swear this oath on behalf of all who are in attendance here. And this is the oath that he must swear:

That no one will ever raise hostilities against this place and against the people who gather here, and if anyone else does so, we will all stop them from harming it and them.

Now listen to how you must perform the sacrifice for this oath.

You have, in your house, a tripod with bronze legs. It is like the one that Heracles dedicated to the Pythian's shrine, at Delphi, after he had devastated the city of Troy and before he had set off on another mission.

Over this tripod, cut the throats of three sheep—although today you may substitute bloodless offerings. Then, on the inside, in the hollow of the tripod's belly, inscribe the oath. When you've done this, give the tripod to the God who rules the shrine, to keep for the eyes of the whole community, as a witness and a reminder of the oath.

Those are my words to you, Theseus.

Theseus:
Lady Athena, I shall do as you say and hope that you correct my every error. *(Indicating the king.)* I will bind this man with an oath.

Athena, be our guide because when you are with us, the community cannot go wrong and will stay safe for ever.

adapted from Euripides, *Suppliant Women*, 1180-1231

Exit Athena.

Theseus summons attendants who bring forward wine in a libation vessel, a tripod with the oath written on it: "No one will ever raise hostilities against this place and against the people who gather here, and if anyone else does so, we will all stop them from harming it and them". Also they bring the three loaves in a basket and a sharp knife. One attendant with the wine stands next to another IER, one next to Theseus and another attendant stands next to the King with a script to help him say the oath correctly. One stands with the tripod and one or more with the "sheep".

Theseus: King, approach!
The king of the place proceeds to centre of ritual circle and faces the people.
Now swear this oath before us all:

"No one will ever raise hostilities against this place and against the people who gather here, and if anyone else does so, we will all stop them from harming it and them".

King: As king of this place, I swear before the Gods and the people of this place, that no one will ever raise hostilities against this place and against the people who gather here, and if anyone else does so, we will all stop them from harming it and them.

My people and friends: Why own a spear and use it to destroy, to kill each other? Stop! And when you've given up your war, guard quietly your cities in tranquility. A little thing is life, but we should spend it well.

Euripides, *Suppliant Women*: lines 940-944

We can't bring back a mortal life; wealth we can recover.

Euripides, *Suppliant Women*, line 769

Attendants come forward with the tripod and "sheep". One at a time, Theseus slices a piece off each sheep/bread over the tripod and drops it into the urn. As they sacrifice the "victims", women ululate, stopping after the last "animal" is slaughtered. The attendants then take the "sheep/bread" away to be sliced into many small bits for distribution after the ritual.

IERs then fill three libation bowls or cups with wine and hand to IER, Theseus and King.

IER (*holding libation bowl toward heaven*):
To Athena!
O Mother of arts, who brings …
Rage to the wicked and wisdom to the good …
Purger of evils, all-victorious queen,
Hear us, O Goddess, when to thee we pray
With supplicating voice both night and day,
And at the right seasons, give peace and health,
And being ever present, bring aid to those who honor you,
O, much implored, bright-eyed inventor of the arts ..

from *Orphic Hymn 32* to Athena

We dedicate these offerings to you!
IER pours libation onto the ground.

Theseus (*holding libation bowl toward heaven*):
To Athena!
He pours a libation onto the ground.

King (*holding libation bowl toward heaven*):

To Athena!
He pours a libation onto the ground.

The attendant pours remaining wine into the tripod. At some point, one IER will empty the wine and bread into secluded ground where it will not be disturbed.

DELTA: Libation to the Modern Heroes

IER refills a libation vessel - a small jug - with milk.

IER (*holding libation vessel and free hand towards earth*):
Sometimes, also, the forces of nature assault us, as well as accidents and other unforeseen events. Where do we find the strength to put our own well-being aside to protect all we love? How do we find the courage to put our lives on the line? Even when we know we must protect what is more important and more enduring than ourselves, fear may hold us back.

The ancients realized that the strength to defend comes from a divine source and that the ability to ignore our personal survival and to see beyond our small part in the universe is not an ordinary human trait. Today, we honour all those who have shown the divinely given traits of strength and self-discipline and self-sacrifice; we honour the people who have shouldered the responsibility to protect and defend us: members of the defense forces, the fire departments, the police departments and first responders of all types.

To the Heroes!

Pours libation onto ground.

EPSILON: Conclusion and Blessings

IER: Then may blessings go with you, and may the Gods watch benevolently over you and guard you with favourable fortunes!
Aeschylus, Libation Bearers, lines 1063-4

IER: O Gods, may it be so for us!
All: O Gods, may it be so for us!
Sophocles, Philoctetes, lines 779ff

IERs distribute the portions of the ritual offering (bread). All recess from the fire pit toward the feasting location to the sound of drums, music, singing and dancing.

- - - - - - - - - - Ω - - - - - - - - - -

Pronunciation of Names

Capitalized syllables are emphasized.

Theseus .... THE-se-us
Periphetes .... per-ee-FEE-tees
Sinis .... SEE-nees
Krommyonian .... kro-mee-O-nee-an
Pallas .... PA-las
Erechtheus .... e-REK-the-us
Aegeus.......................... E-ge-us
Minotaur .... MEE-no-tar
Attica............................ AT-tee-ca
Minos .... MEE-nos
Knossos .... kno-SOS
Ariadne .... a-ree-AD-nee
Pythian .... pee-THEE-an
Delphi: .... DEL-fee

Melissa Gold has been involved with ancient Hellenic Spirituality since 2003. A mother and grandmother, Melissa retired from teaching in 2001 to study Ancient Greek and classical antiquity at university before helping to found Hellenic Spirit in Toronto in 2009. Now working in IT for an online learning company, Melissa leads rituals and special events based on ancient Greek texts and scholarship. In communication with followers of this spiritual path in Greece, Melissa is also studying to obtain clergy status in the US organization Hellenion and has served on the Prytaneia (board) for that organization. Amazingly, she still finds time for long-distance cycling and recently took part in the Ride to Conquer Cancer. (Contact Melissa and Hellenic Spirit at hellenicspiritcanada@gmail.com. Hellenion web site: http://hellenion.org)

THE HEDGEWITCH AND THE HURRICANE

by Juniper Birch

As we huffed and puffed our way up the soggy path to the Vé, carrying bags, boxes and a large wicker chair, Grey and I joked about how this is exactly the sort of thing they don't tell you in Pagan 101 books. The behind the scenes work you never think of when attending a ritual. Carrying a massive, heavy chair over swampy ground while being eaten alive by all manner of bugs.

After Grey left me alone in Vé, I set about setting up. Laying out the altar, lighting candles, all that stuff. I must have exited and then entered the Vé a dozen times during my preparations. At first I properly curtsied and said "Hail!" each time. Then after about the fourth rendition, I switched to my old standard, how I greet the spirits that reside with my own craft room "Hey guys!" or "Back again" or "Knock knock." But finally I simply gave it up entirely. They were watching, those Gods in the poles. They knew what I was up to. I chatted at them the entire time, telling them every silly little random thought that entered my mind as I worked until there was nothing more to tell Them. With my preparations complete, now began the wait.

It's a rather uncomfortable thing, to realize you have to pee while in the woods, outside a sacred site, with no restroom nearby. I moved into the bushes as far away from the Vé as I dared to go, and found myself wondering how many völvas and the like throughout history had snuck off to empty their bladders before the folk arrived for a mind-blowing ritual? I glanced sideways at the God-poles standing tall, barely seen over the weeds I squatted in. I grinned up at Frigg's pole. "All of them, at some point, I bet!" More things they don't tell you about, or they simply don't think about.

The sun set and the mosquitoes came out. Birds sang and the small creatures of the forest skittered about in the tree limbs. I pondered the stuff they don't tell you as I stood outside the Vé, leaning against the weapon rack, smoking a cigarette.

My black princess satin robe with black eyelet over-robe had bell sleeves that had been hemmed short to avoid catching fire – one of the things they DO tell you. But the hem of the robe's skirting was rather long. Perfect for prancing about in a temple room, wearing shoes (the better if heels) but barefoot or sandaled in an outdoor Vé? Not so much. Ah well, I would just have to watch my footing and hold the skirting up a bit. Nothing to do about it now. Not with the folk soon to be on their way, and me squeezed into a fancy robe that is so snug it takes a coven to get me in and out of it.

One thing they don't tell you about is the wait. Ritual space has been prepared. Candles have been lit. Incense burning. The witch has been carefully squeezed into her elaborate robe. Now, the wait. The wait can ruin you if you let it. Butterflies begin to form in your belly. The what-ifs reach insidious tendrils into your mind, spreading fear and doubt.

The wind will blow out the candles. The bugs will be so ferocious that it will ruin the mood. You'll trip over that stupid robe. They are all going to laugh at you. Frigg will refuse to ride you, refuse to answer questions, refuse the offerings. The high seat, which is really just a wicker chair, doesn't look like a high seat, it looks like a wicker chair.

The wait will ruin you, if you let it.

So I didn't focus on the wait. I focused on the coming storm. I could feel it there, gathering at the edge of Vé, gathering around Her newly raised God-pole. I could feel it gathering at the edge of my own mind. The storm that I was to call, to invite, to invoke, to summon, to funnel into my own head and unleash within.

I finished my cigarette and stepped back into the Vé. With careful steps I approached Frigg's God-pole. I wrapped my arms around the pole and rested my head against it. I repeated each step of the ritual out loud, three times.

I knew she was listening. The storm was gathering. I whispered words to her that I would repeat later during the ritual: Frigg, I ask you to do this thing, not for my own ego. Not so I can impress my friends. I ask you to do this for the folk. These folk who honour you. Who study and research and read the lore to learn about you. These folk who talk about you and share your stories. These folk who sing your praises and give offerings to you. These folk who have gathered here this weekend, who have carved this pole and raised it. Do it for these folk who seek your wisdom and guidance. They deserve it. Please.

The gathering storm is even stronger now. I can feel Her within the God-pole I lean against. Waiting, watching. I hear steps coming down the path to the Vé. Deliberately loud so as not to surprise me. "That'll be Auz," I whisper.

Amusement and mischief run down and through the God-pole . I find myself grinning. "Shall we make him wait then, Lady?" I ask.

Yes. She seems to be in a playful mood. So we ignore the steps and wait until he politely clears his throat. With a final pat, I step away from the God-pole . It's time to take our places, the folk will be coming soon. The ritual to begin.

I am clumsy and awkward throughout the first part of the ritual. The storm is building and it takes away my ability to focus on the here and now. Grey acts as my handmaiden and without her I would have been lost. My concentration is on the coming storm. I drop something once and another time find myself accidentally reaching into the thrunble, my fingers touching the red-hot incense coals, my fingers come out black and sooty, yet they feel no heat. No burns, though there should have been. Her storm is building and she is protecting me.

I step up to the altar and make my offerings, promising more at the end of the ritual if all goes well. I entreat her. I speak the words I had so carefully practiced before. Now I am in the calm before the storm. My ability to sense energy and the unseen has become deaf-blind. All I feel is a nearly painful anticipation. As Gandalf would say: the deep breath before the plunge. I am told later by the folk that they felt the energy in the Vé pulse outwards with each sentence as I entreated Her and begged her for participation. I sense nothing. I feel nothing. If she has acquiesced to my request, I do not know.

I step up to the God-pole anyway. I rest my hands upon it and lean my forehead against the smooth wood. Touch it with my third eye. I breathe. Grey teaches the folk my power song, to help me enter into trance. They begin to sing.

I find the storm again, gathering around and within the God-pole . Adjusting my stance, holding up the hem of my damnable robe with one hand, I begin to circle the God-pole, wrapping my hand and arm around it for balance and connection. After the first couple of slow and careful rotations I begin to worry. I'm totally going to trip. Earlier Grey had warned me to be careful as I spun around the pole, the last thing we needed was for me to fall and brain myself on Odin's pole standing right beside Frigg's. I'm uncoordinated in trance. One reason why I generally don't do trance-dancing around the fire, I simply dance. Ah but walking, and this spinning around a pole or tree, this works for me, so long as I don't trip. I bite my lip in concern.

Just then I feel a hand cover my mine, clasping me gently to the pole. Steadying me. Guiding me. She wasn't about to let me fall. Trustingly I spin. I spin and I spin around the pole widdershins. Gradually taking faster and firmer steps. I close my eyes and focus on the storm within.

I have no sense as to whether my steps take on a rhythm. I do not think they matched the odd beat of the song the folk sang to me. The words of the chant are difficult to wrap your mouth around. The chant doesn't rhyme, the meter doesn't quite match up. But it has certain words that can be triggers for me and a certain urgency needed for the occasion. An odd and awkward song for an odd and awkward witch.

I breathe deeply. My feet pound the earth. I spin around the pole. Chaos rages in my mind, a swirling mess of a thing. Unfettered and unhinged. Thoughts cannot fully form before they are swept away in the storm. Ring-a-ring a-widdershins, whirlin' skirlin' widdershins. The storm inside builds momentum, matching the quickening pace of my feet. I spin at a pace that feels dangerous. I am held fast by that spectral hand. A greater storm, a hurricane, rages above and within the God-pole itself. My insignificant little human mind does it's best to match, a tempest in a tea-cup. Here we go round the mulberry bush, so early in the morning. I am stretched thin, pulled by the spiraling forces outwards. My consciousness swirls at the edge of myself, expanding outwards. I spin even faster, the chanting is louder. I throw my head back, then down. Ring-a-round the rosy, pocket full of posy. The sound of the folks chanting has become a distant thing, overshadowed by the rushing in my ears. My little storm slips just beyond the confines of mind and body, swirling at the threshold, neither without nor within. It brushes against the hurricane that is Frigg. Electric. Wild. Not as force of nature, but a force of the multiverse. I can comprehend Her as well and an ant can understand my foot. I could just let go completely, surrender. My little storm would be swept away into the maelstrom like a crow feather in a hurricane. Ashes, ashes we all fall down.

Enough. I'm not sure which one of us decides. But it is enough. I halt, bringing my other arm around the pole, facing it again. Returning to my original position.

I am not dizzy.

I have reached the calm after the storm. After the rain has washed away the detritus, the wind has blown away the debris. Now the smell of freshness after the rain. The brilliant quality of sunlight after the clouds move on. The clean crisp feeling in the air after a summer thunder-storm has passed by.

Perfect, painful clarity of mind. A spreading out and in of consciousness. With my now heightened senses I am aware of everything within the Vé. Sharp as a tack, clear as a new day.

This is what lies beyond ecstasy. When one has not strayed from their body.

I am a clean vessel. A hollow bone.

Grey moves towards me silently and gently takes my arm. I disengage from the God-pole and allow her to lead me to the high seat. I land in it pretty hard. Such an uncoordinated witch. Ah, well.

Grey teaches the folk the next song. The chant to call Frigg within. For a moment I lean my head back and open my eyes to gaze at the stars. Their beauty is to grounding, to real, so I close my eyes again and turn my focus inward once more.

As the folk take up the chant, Grey begins to dress me. A shawl, draperies, a dish in my lap, spindle in hand, distaff in the other, and a veil over my head. I am only dimly aware of this happening. Instead, I am reaching for the door.

Somewhere, deep inside, where the mind, the soul and the body meet there is a door. A quiet little backdoor. I do not know if everyone has this door. I do not know if everyone can find it. I do not know if everyone could open it. I do not know if anyone could close it back up again. I *do* know it wouldn't be safe for most people to try.

I can't tell you where to find it. I was shown the backdoor by a very different God than the one who I was about to invite in.

Reaching back, I find the door and cautiously open it. Standing on the threshold, I call out an invitation. This way, this way, here I am. Come in and be welcome.

Grey ties a cord of red linen (that I have spun with my drop spindle) around my neck, runs it the length between the high seat and the God-pole and then ties the other end around the pole. An umbilical. A pathway. A noose. I hang from the God-pole and wait.

Are you there Frigg? It's me Juniper.

I step aside from the backdoor and press myself against the very wall of myself. Making room for her. I wait. I am unsure if she is coming. I have never invited this Goddess in before, never been Her horse, Her hollow bone. With others, there was a rush. An entitled barging in, helping themselves. Pushing me aside so that I have nearly no control, no awareness, little say in the proceedings.

Frigg was so gentle, so delicate that I wasn't sure She had come at all…until She laughed, using my voice. A raw, rough cackle of a laugh escaped my lips. It startled me and I think it startled Grey who was standing beside the high seat, reciting words to entice the Goddess.

I felt Her there, filling me. She didn't shove me down to some half oblivion. She didn't put blinders over Her horse's eyes. She let me stay aware and awake. Pressed up against the wall of myself, out of way but welcome.

Grey steps away from the high seat and assumes her position between the seat and the side altar. She says something, but I can't recall what it was. I was preoccupied with the hurricane. Getting used to Her in me, as She was getting used to being in me.

My mouth worked silently a few times. My tongue rolled around in my mouth. It's a strange thing, to stand back and witness another get accustomed to using your face. It was only a few seconds, but it seemed like an eternity.

"We should say something, to get the ball rolling," I suggested.

I could feel Her consider what to say.

"What do you WANT?" tore from my throat. Still rough, still getting used to using my voice.

I think Grey was taken aback. I think Frigg found this incredibly amusing. My face contorted into a rictus grin. I was glad the for the veil.

Grey asked Frigg something. Asking permission to go ahead with the questioning.

I think it took a few moments to get a response, as at that time She decided She wanted use of my hands. Since She was being such a gracious guest and had actually asked politely to have use of my upper body, I agreed that would be fine.

She waved one hand around, inexpertly. "Very well"

So it began.

My memory of the actual questioning is spotty. Dreamlike. I remember some parts very clearly and others not at all. For example, at some point someone gave an apple as an offering. I have no memory of this at all. I only know an apple was given because after the ritual was done, I found bits of apple stuck in my teeth. I asked Grey and she confirmed: someone had indeed given an apple.

Some offerings I remember and others I do not. In some cases I remember who gave what, but mostly I'm unsure which person gave which offering. I know that She liked mead more than ale or beer (but She still really enjoyed the ale and beer). Frigg was very interested in hand/home-made items; She seemed to approve of them quite a bit. One person gave a very personal and valued object, a true sacrifice, and She was deeply touched.

I also learned that Frigg loves plums. One of the folk gave a plum (along with something else). She approved of the gifts, answered the question and then as the person was going back to their seat, Frigg suddenly wanted more plums. She was about to open my mouth and demand more plums. In an instant I had to go from polite host leaning against the back wall, idly watching the proceedings, to stern little Hedgewitch. "No. Not right now. People are waiting to ask their questions. I'll let the whole world know you like plums, there will be more plums in the future".

Can you tell a Goddess "NO"? Do you have the strength of will to tell a Goddess, *who is currently inside of you "no"*? Do you have the strength of will to tell a Goddess, who is currently inside of you, that they can't have something they want? Knowing that if you pissed them off enough, that

Goddess could tear your mind, your soul, to pieces in an instant?

This is where is gets really, truly dangerous. Bloody, stupidly dangerous. I've heard about it, read about it, seen it with my own eyes. While it is something that may be spoken of and written about, it seems that it is one of those things they don't often tell you about. Or maybe it is one of those things that people tell you about, but many folks just don't listen.

People acting as a horse for a God who demands more and more alcohol, leaving the horse with alcohol poising by the end of it.

People who let a God in and awaken the next morning sticky, naked, and lying beside someone who they never would have consented to have sex with. Wondering if a condom had been used, wondering what had happened, and if that was the only person.

Gods who, once in, refuse to leave until a certain offering is made to them, causing the people in attendance to scramble around, possibly having to rush to a store or other person's house to find it.

Gods who once inside and approached by someone they dislike, by someone who disbelieves in that God, or by someone who lies to their horse's face, and are then kicked or hit. Much to the horror of the attendees and the horse.

The Gods are dangerous. They can destroy you in an instant. Inside of me, brushing up against my mind and spirit, Frigg could have dealt me serious damage with a single lashing.

The Gods are powerful. I met a God once who upon seeing me torn asunder in the underworld, put me back together again with the ease of a well-practiced father reattaching a doll's head to its body. And then demanded a price for His services.

I know of someone who once cut down a tree sacred to the Gods, by mistake. Shortly afterwards he died suddenly of a brain aneurysm. His spouse was driven insane with grief.

I know of someone who lied under oath to his Elders, swearing by Odin as he did so. He was shortly after hit by a truck, his body broken. While he laid in traction, his wife left him. Being in the USA, the hospital bills caused him to lose what the wife did not take with her. Later, he confessed his lie to his Elders and over the next while, found love again, found a good job and rebuilt his life.

I know someone who once promised Freya that she would sacrifice a rabbit to her. A difficult gift for a vegan. She put it off, and put it off. Until she started dreaming of rabbits. She poured an expensive wine into a beautiful wooden bowl, asking Freya to accept this offering instead. The next morning the bowl had been split in half, where it lay, the wine ruining the altar cloth, as flies buzzed around it.

More than once, I have been penniless, jobless and living under another's roof and hospitality. Exhausted, depressed, and feeling hopeless.

Walking on blistered feet, desperately searching for a job in a strange city. A homeless man with one black eye swollen shut, a long grey beard and a cane asked me for spare change. I gave him half of my last dollars. And shortly after, I found a job, a home and my way in a new city.

It's one of those things people don't like to talk about. How the Gods are bigger than us. So much MORE than us. How dangerous and difficult and capricious and troublesome they can be. We want the Gods to be our friends. Many people I know want to feel as if they are on equal footing as the Gods. They refuse to consider having something in the universe bigger and stronger than they are.

We want an all-knowing, all-loving, omnipresent super Goddess who changes everything she touches and everything she touches changes. Who never, ever, gets angry with us, because She is beyond anger, or hate or spite.

Never mind what the lore tells us. Gods who rape. Gods who kill. Gods who lie, cheat, and steal. Gods who lash out in jealously. Gods who betray their kin. Gods who impulsively give up their sword for a nice piece of ass, and thus must fight the battle at the end of all things with an antler in hand.

Those are just myths, of course. They don't mean anything. Except when they do.

I try to talk to people about how the Gods are so powerful, so awesome and greater-than. How terrifying they can be. I'm usually just misunderstood. Perhaps I do not articulate it well enough. Perhaps people just don't want to think about it.

Perhaps most people never experience these things, because most of us never move beyond the basics. Most of us will never invite the hurricane in our heads. Most of us will never be torn apart by nice little birdies in the underworld and need to make a deal with the Master to get put back together again.

Do you have the balls to tell Frigg that She can't have any more plums? Do you have any idea how much balls and sass it takes to do just that? Do you have any idea how stupidly dangerous it can be?

But …

I've seen it before, read about it and heard about it. One of those things they do tell you about, sometimes. If during such a rite, you just start giving the God anything they demand, they will keep demanding. Rituals derailed as everyone scrambles to find more plums, and then have to sit there for an hour as they watch Frigg eat a bag of plums. Holding a horse's hair away from her face while she pukes up a belly full of plums. You can ask them to take away the drunkenness, or make sure the horse doesn't get sick from eating a pound of plums. Sometimes they will do just that.

It's a risk you have to be willing to take when you do this kind of work. The chance you might find yourself with battered and bruised feet, a sick stomach full of plums, a wicked hangover, an STD because the God riding you decided to screw someone. You also have to be willing and able to say no, if you can. Maybe they won't listen, maybe they will get pissed off and lash out, maybe they will just leave, maybe you'll ruin your relationship with them for good. Maybe you'll wind up a poet, a witch, a madman, or dead.

You have to be able to calculate the risks. If you aren't willing to accept the risks, don't do this kind of work. It's okay to decide it's not for you.

So I told Frigg no more plums. Thankfully, She was okay with that. Such a *nice* Goddess. The next person came up to ask their question and She was back on task, the plums forgotten. Thank goodness Gods are often easily distracted. No more mead for you…here have a shiny thing!

Sometimes She was more present, and sometimes I was more present. Hence the spotty memory, I suppose. I remember some of the questions and not others. Like the offerings, in many cases I remember a question but not which person asked it. Or I remember a person coming up to the high seat, but not the question they asked.

Once a person had asked their question, they chose a few pieces from my casting collection and placed them in the bowl in our lap. Together we read the augury. I know my set well enough to recognize the pieces by feel, even the polished stones. A very interesting thing, that I will ponder and utilize, is that She had a slightly different take on the meanings/symbolism of a few of the pieces. Her impressions of them were similar but not quite the same.

There were cases where only one piece really mattered, others where each piece mattered. Cases where the pieces only reinforced what She already was going to say. Cases where She read the pieces and then added something else as well.

Watching Frigg use my set was very educational and I'm glad I chose to go that route. Typically, you don't use a divinatory device during such a rite, the God simply answers the questions. They already know the answer. However, my set is very important to me, and a major part of my practice. I figured that if She wasn't interested in it, She would ignore it. Her willingness to use it, Her approval of it, and Her showing me different interpretations of some of the pieces was very rewarding!

A lot of folks had a hard time finding the bowl in our lap. It was very dark. I'm told that the darkness surrounding the high seat grew even deeper whenever Frigg was strongest in me. A few people struggled to find the bowl, a couple missed it entirely, but She was patient. At one point She picked up the bowl and waved it around a bit, I think to help the questioner find it.

One piece from the set kept being chosen, over and over again. Thorn. The little stick of hawthorn, shaped like a stang. Sometimes She ignored the piece and sometimes She read it. I began to worry the bag wasn't be shaken well enough, so in response, She pointed one imperious finger at Grey and commanded her to shake the bag. Still, Thorn kept coming up. A message for me? A message for the group? Both? A strange coincidence? I do not know. More to meditate on. In my set Thorn is used to symbolize witchcraft, magick, the cunning arts and so forth. Though amongst a bunch of Heathens, Thorn could take on a slightly different meaning.

Eventually, everyone who dared to had come before the high seat. Grey asked Frigg if She was done. In response, She knocked my stang/distaff over. Grey and I had agreed that if at any point, I needed the ritual to end, I would knock down the distaff. If I could, if I had enough control to do so. I don't recall explaining this to Frigg, but being in my head, She knew.

So they thanked Frigg and hailed Her. The chant asking Her to leave me was sung. Grey cut the cord and began to remove my draperies. I lost all thought and consciousness as She left me. She went as gently as She came and it almost felt like dozing off on a lazy summer afternoon.

I heard my friends calling my name. Calling me back. I struggled toward the sound of their voices, slowing spreading myself back within myself. Filling my own vessel once again. Suddenly, Grey pulled off the veil I wore. It was like when your mother rips the blankets off the bed, to wake you, on a cold morning. I must have made a very unhappy face! It was less than pleasant and suddenly very cold. Mental note for next time: always tell you handmaiden to SLOWLY remove the veil! However it did the trick, and with a few groans and stretches I was back properly in my body, my mind fairly settled. I was back amongst the folk.

"Hey Juni" Grey said tenderly, as she bent over me.

"Hey" I said back and leaned forward for a hug.

Then I said: "I have to pee".

Juniper Birch just happened to move to Ontario around the time that Raven's Knoll was acquired. Since then she has volunteered her time and effort to support the campground and many of the events that are held there, including organizing and running The Witches' Sabbat at Raven's Knoll. Beyond this, Juniper has run blogs and podcasts on Paganism and witchcraft and published a variety of articles on these subjects. Juniper has contributed to two anthologies: "To Fly by Night" published by Pendraig, and "Hoofprints in the Wildwood" published by Gullinbursti Press.

ABIDING AT THE KNOLL

by Reverend Auz

A version of this chapter first appeared in "The Dudespaper: A Lifestyle Magazine for the Deeply Casual," on November 10, 2014.

Brothers and sisters! We have heard the Word, and it is "Abide." The Raven's Knoll congregation of the Church of the Latter-Day Dude held a tent revival to learn from, and apply, the teachings of the Dude. The first LebowskiCampFest was held from August 9 to 10, 2014 at Raven's Knoll. This fest is a campout where we commune with the wisdom of the movie The Big Lebowski on the weekend after the August long weekend.

Raven's Knoll is home to Canada's largest Pagan gathering, the Kaleidoscope Gathering (KG), held around the August long weekend every year. The Pagan community in Canada is really laid back and recognizes a good ethos when they see it. Around these parts, over the years, the theology of Discordianism has been popular, as has the Church of the Sub-Genius. But now that we have heard the word of the Church of the Latter Day Dude, the evolution of introspective hilarity and slack has reached its logical theological zenith. Although LebowskiCampFest was established as a weekend for volunteer staff to chill after KG, it was indeed created by a bunch of event organizers. Thus, like a Dude getting wrapped up in events beyond his control, we could not help but organize lots of awesome stuff to do.

The opening ceremony on Friday evening was a "Suitcase Toss." Adventures begin in the simplest ways. Ours, like that of our Prophet, started with a simple tossing of a suitcase filled with undergarments. Everyone had a chance to throw the Ringer, either from the campground's golf cart or from Reverend Myst's motorized wheelchair.

We felt that everyone needed to get prettied up like Bunny, so there was then the opportunity to get "Green Pedicures" from Reverend Dood B. Here and Reverend Brynn. Toenails should be green. Hedonism demands it.

That evening, after people had set up their camp and had a few beverages, we collected everyone together and stepped away from the campfire into the darkness. As you know, there is no sweeter sound in all existence than the song of whales (except maybe the sound of bowling). Whales are the opposite of the Eagles, man. Our evening rite involved joining Reverend Auz to listen to the songs of the humpbacked whale while meditating on readings from the second sacred text of Dudeism, "The Dude De Ching." Everyone turned their eyes towards the shining vault of stars above our heads and we cranked 20 minutes of whale songs at full volume to fill the forest with their relaxing, mournful trilling and clicks, as we contemplated the wisdom of Taoism as digested through limber minds and the tropes of the Cohen brothers.

On Saturday morning we arose at the crack of noon. As Dudeists we recognize that a place is a home when you have a rug to really tie things together. Priests of Lebowski, Reverend Dood and Reverend Brynn, took Achievers into the woods to arrange rugs, to come to an understanding that all of the world can be the home of a dude. We had a bit of fun doing a photo shoot with everyone and voted on the best costume. Apostate Gypsy won the costume contest with his excellent renditions of The Stranger, Buddy Face Down in the Muck, and Walter. (Not only were his costumes great, but like a good friend of Dudeism, he ensured there was a Trinity of them.) The most popular costume amongst Achievers was the bathrobe of the Dude and of Maude. In fact, some people are still wearing them, I think. The best costume winner received two prizes: the acclaim of the Achievers and a saintly bottle of homemade coffee liqueur from whence the sacred draught is mixed.

Even if there are no lanes, a Dude can still bowl. Never quit the tournament, even if you have no lanes! It is by struggle with our foes and interactions with our inner narrator that we learn what is truly possible. During the daytime a few of us did a little "Cowboy Bowling" while drinking some oat sodas, while Lebowski-ites looks on. We felt that this was only fair. In the movie, the Stranger has to watch all the bowling, but never plays. So, we played horseshoes, which is kind of like the outdoor equivalent of bowling. At the very least, it put us in a Dude frame of mind.

Our local congregation of the Church of the Latter Day Dude has been influenced by the traditional teachings of the Holy Spirit Association for the Unification of World Dudeism (commonly known at the "Dudeification Church" or in the media as "The Doodies"). So it was natural that we held a mass ordination of Dudeist priests. Everyone took the oath from "The Abide Guide" together, at the same time, right beside the Travelling Shrine of our Perpetual Dude. Reverend Dᴑᴑð, Arch-Deacon of Swedish Log Bowling, then printed out ordination certificates for eighteen new priests and priestesses of the Church of the Latter-Day Dude.

All of this was rather thirsty work, so we proceeded on to "Sacramental White Russian Mixology & Tasting." Praise the mixing of the opposites – opaque and clear, hot coffee and cold ice, white and black, stimulant and depressant. As we all know, the White Russian is the sacramental drink of Dudeism. Priests of the Church of the Latter Day Dude, Reverend Dood B. Here and Reverend Doug, held a service to demonstrate how to make coffee liqueur from scratch and how to mix the perfect White Russian or closely related beverage. People brought their own ingredients and shared them, creating the "White Pirate" with coconut milk and rum for the lactose intolerant to "Blind Russian," using Bailey's instead of cream. No matter what the Interwebz or bar guides say, we Canadian Dudeists decry that using goat's milk does not a "White Canadian" make. It was the consensus that a true "White Canadian" is made from coffee liqueur, half and half, and maple syrup whiskey liqueur.

To get us warmed up for the movie, Reverend Wolfsong and Reverend Earthsong of the Official Church Choir of the Latter Day Dudes organized a Creedence Clearwater karaoke concert. Renditions of CCR were the main focus of the concert, where most people in the crowd participated at some point. (There may have been a few other tunes sung that inspired the first draft of the Port Huron Statement. But, there was definitely no Eagles played. We all hate the fucking Eagles, man.)

The heart of every LebowskiCampFest is the illuminating wisdom of the big screen. The secrets reside within. The layers of meaning go deeper and deeper as one's understanding of the movie "The Big Lebowski" expands. Only through abiding at a screening and in contemplation afterwards is it revealed. We thank Jackie Treehorn and the Lost Dominion Screening Collective for arranging to show the movie. (The big debate was whether or not Donnie was part of Walter's mind or an individual biological being in his own right. You can imagine the conversations about the nature of reality that followed.)

After the movie was finished someone set up "Night Bowling." We used a fluorescent volleyball as the ball, sets of fairy lights as lane markers, and put glow sticks in plastic pop bottles full of water for pins. It was exceedingly trippy, man.

The Achievers eventually congregated around the bonfire. (Jackie Treehorn knows what people want at a party, eh?) Their minds were getting limber and the conversation was flowing. Into that reverie, Reverend Zau the Nihilist reminded everyone of the flip-side of Dudeism by leading people in some "Nihilist Stargazing." The stars are harsh teachers.

Seemingly happy and twinkling they are actually light that comes from exploding collections of matter that died billions of years before our world was even created. We people are just a tiny speck in all that existence, that existence that ends without hearing our thoughts or recognizing our efforts. Reverend Zau the Nihilist read a selection of existentialist philosophy to everyone while they contemplated the futility and nothingness in the vastness of the starry sky.

Throughout the weekend, the Raven's Knoll food truck was selling a very special menu. In honour of the Big Lebowski, the menu, included: lingonberry waffles, In-und-Aus burgers, pigs in the blanket, and Ralph's coffee. (At the request of the Little Lebowski Urban Achievers, people in attendance also donated non-perishable food items to the local food bank.)

On Sunday, everyone had to pack up to go home. To end the event a "Scattering of the Cremains" ceremony was held. At the end of the adventure, there is always still a chance to be with friends one last time and remember the good times. Our closing ceremony, as taught by the example of our Prophet, was an ending with memories shared around the scattering of cremains (in this case, the ashes from our communal campfire).

The event was a great success and other LebowskiCampFests have happened since. Each year a new theme is selected, be it "Art is Strongly Vaginal" or "Dream Sequences." Every event is little different, with new ins-and-outs and what-have-yous. (The Maude-ist Aerial Painting while flying on a zip line to create a communal Jackson Pollock style painting proved particularly popular, and people loved the Dudeist Wedding.) Each year the activities are a bit different, but the event will definitely include a "Ringer Toss," "Mass Ordination," movie screening, and "Scattering of the Cremains" every year.

Mark it eight, Dude.

Abide.

Reverend Auz is part of household that travels in cars with license plates that read "ABID3S" and "MARKIT0." He keeps his mind limber by learning about many different religions and philosophies. He completes a Rubik'sCube™ by deconstructing it, then reconstructing it again.

AN ODE TO THE KNOLL

by Rae Green

A friend dragged me, to unplug, one Canada Day long past.
Rituals of sun soaked afternoons in hammocks and in the river.
Cider soaked evenings, joining in tumultuous bardic, song and drum.

Very soon, I found that I could not stay away.
Work weekends, menu planning, packing lists.
Pitching tents in rain, and dark. Early morning giggles.

So many rituals of my life have happened since.
A partner and I walk to see the Crone in the darkest night.
Tokens exchanged, gifts of knowledge imparted, kisses for old Horny.

A Beltaine braid under a sunny sky, on hot sands.
Lovers chase each other through the woods. Sing Praise Brigit!
A baby cries new as the light turns to Imbolc.

We place tiny feet on the ground, introducing new life.
Dancing with daughters; tracing their first steps around our Red Spiral.
Our son, learned a bicycle in a weekend, safely on the duff.

Sinking stones, singing Mermish songs.
Pass the drum circle and Hail to the King.
Stand with Loki, who never minds if you do a J.

Late night Caucasians, faulty ball return in the alley.
I scatter his cremains to the wind.
You're out of your element; I Abide.

Solitary walks through the Witches Spiral,
building with community, growing my family.
Throwing axes, flashlight tag, My M.A.

Hail to Ravens. Hail to the Vé.
Plans for growth, more summers to come.
Hail to the Knoll.

Rae Green lives in Ottawa with her lovely partners, her many children, cats, and a largish dog, and spends her summers trying to escape the city for the tranquility of the Knoll.

FIRST FOOTING OF
WENDELL AND LORETTA

by Sheena MacIsaac, with Rae Green

I am a member of the modern Druid group Ár nDraíocht Féin: A Druid Fellowship (ADF), and am Head Druid of the Ottawa Grove, Lake of Oaks. Raven's Knoll is an important place for us in ADF; we hold our yearly regional meeting at the Knoll and treasure the fellowship, discussion, and ritual we participate in there. ADF Druidry celebrates the eight-fold celebratory year with public rituals and additional special rites both marking group activity (like the Unity Ritual at the regional meeting) and specific rituals within a grove. ADF is largely interested in scholarship and ideas; only the most general of beliefs are mandated (belief in numerous Gods, for example). So congruity between groves is not maintained by identical dogma but by all of the groves using the same definitive order of ritual, although the words and theatrics vary. Our grove, Lake of Oaks, also uses dedicated poetics for the unchanging parts of the ritual (called the 'core order of ritual') and only a minimal amount of spoken word at all. The only Gaelic we use in ritual is the Irish Gaelic "Bíodh sé amhlaidh!" which means 'Let it be so!' as an underlining of intent and a statement of solidarity by all the participants together.

Our particular grove has held two very special rituals at the Knoll: the First-Footings (that is, the first time a baby's bare feet touch the earth) for the last three members. I will present the ritual of Wendell and Loretta's First-Footing (footed together because they were born hardly more than two weeks apart) section by section, explaining the core order of ritual before-hand and the specific adjustments for the occasion.

- - - - - - - - - - ~ - - - - - - - - - -

Beginning

Druids do not create sacred space; we consider all the universe to be sacred. So rather than encircle and enclose the ritual, we endeavor to bring ourselves into the right attitude to recognize and join with the sacred space already around us by clearing our minds of everyday concerns and acknowledging the ongoing wonder. Then we make a declaration of purpose for the specific ritual we have gathered together to celebrate.

- - - - - - - - - - ~ - - - - - - - - - -

Initiating the Rite

A bell is rung. The opening prayer is spoken by the group as a round.

All:
As it was, as it is, as it shall be--
A blessing of blessings come to thee.

Purification

The Keeper of Sacred Space asperges Wendell's Dad, and then Wendell's Dad asperges the members of the circle collectively in their closest quarters. He first holds up an empty bowl for discarded everyday concerns,

Keeper of Sacred Space:
Here leave behind the ordinary.

Each person touches their bunched fingers to their forehead, then opens their fingers over the bowl. Then each person is aspersed, sprinkled with fluid from the special bowl, in turn.

Be purified, be sained, be merry.

Honouring the Earth-Mother

All sing:
O Thou, our blue and lovely Earth,
We take from you, you give to us.
What can we give of equal worth?
Nothing but love, nothing but trust.

All kiss their hand then place it on the Earth.

Statement of Purpose

Loretta's Mama: Why are we here?

All: We are here to present Wendell and Loretta to the Gods!

Wendell's Momma: As our ancestors once did, so do we do today, and so will our children do in the future. This is their blessing-meet, their first-footing, and the honouring of the Patrons who have watched over them so far and, we petition, will continue to with our thanks and praise.

- - - - - - - - - - ~ - - - - - - - - - -

Middle

Having centered and grounded ourselves and declared our intention, we next direct our gathered energy towards opening a door to the Other World so that we can invite the non-human participants to join us if they wish to. As well, we negotiate a treaty with those beings who are not interested or inimical to the ritual to not participate; we step outside the ritual and offer to those beings (generally grouped as 'Wild Magic' or 'Outdwellers'– not evil but completely outside our human ethical referential) a token of negotiated peace between us.

- - - - - - - - - - ~ - - - - - - - - - -

Creating the Three Worlds: Fire, Well, and Tree

Keeper of Sacred Space:
Let us call up the Three Realms.

O Sacred Well, here flow;
Well up from far below!
From below let it be thus,
Sacred Well, flow in us!

All: Sacred Well, flow in us!

Bring to us Sacred Fire;
Hearts and minds let us aspire.
Flaming, bring us to Imbas,
Sacred Fire, burn in us!

All: Sacred Fire, burn in us!

Unveil yourself, Sacred Tree;
Grow in all Worlds, one in three.
And in ourselves, in perfect trust,
Sacred Tree, grow in us!

All: Sacred Tree, grow in us!

Bíodh sé amhlaidh!

All: Bíodh sé amhlaidh! *("Bee-shay ow-way")*

Acknowledgement of the Outsiders

Outsiders Druid:
Wild Spirits of Opposition,
As were fought at Magh Tuireadh.
Let us here make a condition,
Leave us unharmed, root and twig.

Land Spirits of this Timeless Place,
We, ephemeral as bubbles,
Seek to stand with you in space,
But not to cause you any troubles.

All who do not wish us well,
We ask you to remain outside.
Here is a gift and so farewell,
Peace to you where you abide.

Shows the Outsiders what the offering will be (i.e., opens and sets down the bottle of ale).

Opening the Gate

Gatekeeper:
Crown far above, roots far below,
Trunk here in everyday;
Let the mists part, let the light grow,
Show us the way!

Out onto the sea we row,

By ourselves we'll go astray.
Your guidance and Your wind's flow,
Grant them, Manannán , we pray!

Let the gates be open!
Bíodh sé amhlaidh!

All: Bíodh sé amhlaidh! *("Bee-shay ow-way")*

- - - - - - - - - - ~ - - - - - - - - - -

Invitations

Assuming the gate to the Other World to be open (we will check later), we now issue our invitations. ADF ritual always invites the three Kindreds (Nature Spirits, Ancestors, and Shining Ones) but in this instance the generally invited Kindreds are also specified–the Nature Spirits of Horse and Snake are invited because these are the Chinese astrological signs of the babies, specific Ancestors of the babies are named and the Ancestor that each baby is named after is specially invited, and famous heroes in the ancestral line (or storied people from far back connected to the family) are honoured.

As well as offerings to the Kindreds, this section creates what our grove refers to as 'Magic Juice'; we offer a portion of beverage (variously juice, ale, water, or wine) to the Kindreds in the expectation that they will transform it by their acceptance and we will then share it among ourselves and also with them in fellowship.

- - - - - - - - - - ~ - - - - - - - - - -

Inviting the Three Kindreds …

… Waters

A portion of the drink is poured into the horn when each Kindred Offering is made.

Loretta's Mamas:
Nature Spirits, wild and green,
Come to us from the Between.
All Earth breathes, breathes through us,
Interdependent, always thus.

Thunder up on cart-horse hooves!

Spirit of Brumby, will you come?
And Spirit of Snake, if spirit moves;
Smaller than most, smarter than some.

Come, Spirits, bless us and our kin,
What's just begun and what has been.

Offers wild food to the Nature Spirits and pours a portion of the beverage into the horn.

Loretta's Mama:
With this we offer drink as well,
For you to change with Nature's spell.

… Ancestors

Wendell's Momma:
Stretching back through all the ages,
Here, we have opened up a portal,
Grannies and uncles, knights and sages,
Bring us your help, who once were mortal.

Wendell's Dad:
We remember Wendell from before,
Now the name is used once more.

Loretta's Mama:
We call you, Loretta, from before,
Now the name is used once more.

Wendell's Momma:
Nanny Irene, shield us all from hurt,
Come please with your sister, Uncle Bert.

Wendell's Dad:
Grandfather and Brother, come together,
To keep us from the stormy weather.

Loretta's Mama:
Mother and Daughter stand in this place,
Loretta Mabel, Loretta Agnes: lend your grace!

Offers bread or oatcakes to the Ancestors, and pours a portion of the beverage into the horn.

Wendell's Momma:
With this we offer drink as well,
For You to change with Ancient spell.

… Shining Ones

Wendell's Dad:
Heroes and Gods, please join our rite,
We give you honour as your due.
Lend us a little of your might,
It will return from us to you.

Wendell's Momma:
Conn of the Hundred Battles,
Be your family's strong good knight.

Wendell's Dad:
Black Michael the Lighthouse Keeper,
Guide us with your circling light.

Loretta's Mama:
Barbara and Standish Jones will bring,
Bones and genes and blessings bright.

Offers hazelnuts to the Shining Ones and pours a portion of the beverage into the horn.

Wendell's Dad:
With this we offer drink as well,
For you to change with shining spell.

- - - - - - - - - - ~ - - - - - - - - - -

Deities

As well as the Kindreds (who are always invited), each ritual asks a specific Deity who may be interested in the Working going forward, to whom a grove member or the grove in general is dedicated, or who is connected to the time or place of the ritual, to attend as well. For all of these reasons, Bridget is asked to be present.

- - - - - - - - - - ~ - - - - - - - - - -

Invitation of Beings of the Occasion and Offering to Them

Keeper of the Sacred Space:
Without the Gods, we fail and wither,
With thanks and praise we ask them hither.

Wendell's Momma:
Bridget, bastion of the poor,
Midwife of all those who labour,
For you we open up the door,
Be you now our gracious neighbor.

Wend your way throughout this place,
Bless us with your shining presence.
Enfold these bairns in your embrace,
Send them your grace as birthing present.

Suitable offerings are made.

Prayer of Sacrifice

Wendell's Dad:
High days and everyday as well,
We send the accolades you're due.
In your love then let us dwell,
Send us your grace if pleases you.

We give these gifts with great goodwill,
Our best is what we offer up.
Will you make them better still?
Send blessings down into the cup.

Pours the rest of the offering beverage into the horn.

- - - - - - - - - - ~ - - - - - - - - - -

Working

After the invitations, the Working is done before the grove and Other-Worldly participants. The omen both indicates the presence and support of the Kindreds and Deities and is Their message to us on the specific purpose of the ritual. Thus the Magic Juice, now fully consecrated, is prepared for sharing. In a non-specific ritual this is the place for individual offerings and this ritual acknowledges this but indicates that only the babies are the recipients of the blessings today, as their feet are set on the earth for the first time.

- - - - - - - - - - ~ - - - - - - - - - -

Omen

Here an omen is sought. It is read and described to those present.

Calling for the Blessing

Wendell's Dad:
We thank you in all we say and do,
It's your help keeps us free from strife.
With that care this drink imbue,
Behold the Waters of Life!

Hallowing the Blessing

The blessed horn is mixed back into the shared drink and the hostess sets out a suitable number of individual cups and partly fills them in readiness for the sharing.

Individual Offerings

Guest:
Is it my turn yet?

Loretta and Wendell's Mamas together:
Our babies have a turn today,
This is their First-Footing Rite.
Put your offering away,
Another time will be all right.

Affirmation of the Blessing

Here there is the consecration and sharing of the blessing, where the drink is shared by all who wish partake.

Hostess:
Now is the drink for all to share,
Gods and Spirits, Heroes and mortals.
As we drink we raise a prayer,
Send blessings to us through the portal.

Workings for Loretta and Wendell First-Footing

Loretta's Parents:
We will set your feet to good,
And help you walk the path you should.

Wendell's Parents:
We will try to show you right,
In thought, and heart, and action bright.

- - - - - - - - - - ~ - - - - - - - - - -

Thanking

Now that the Working and the sharing are complete, the human participants thank all of the non-humans for attending, inviting Them to linger or depart as They choose.

- - - - - - - - - - ~ - - - - - - - - -

Thanking the Beings

Wendell's Momma:
Each time we invoke the Powers,
They hear our voices clearer still.
We are Theirs, They are ours,
We each send our great goodwill.
Ours fleeting; Theirs sublime;
From now until the end of time.

Wendell's Dad:
Thanks for Vision, Courage, and Wisdom,

Heroes and Gods, You are our guides.
You show us what we can become.
Please stay with us and here abide.
Thank you, Shining Ones!

All: Thank you, Shining Ones!

Wendell's Momma:
Teach us moderation, piety, hospitality,
Ancestors, those who came before.
Your lives created our reality,
Thanks for staying by the door.
Thank you, Ancestors!

All: Thank you, Ancestors!

Loretta's Mama:
Spirits of Nature, hear our thanks!
As the seasons turn you do what's right,
With fertility, integrity, and perseverance.
Stay with us in dark and light.
Thank you, Nature Spirits!

All: Thank you, Nature Spirits!

Wendell's Momma:
Kindly Bridget, where you tread,
Health and help from pain are spread.
Thank you for coming here today.
We will go and you will stay.

- - - - - - - - - - ~ - - - - - - - - - -

Ending

The human participants now close the gate to the Other World and re-enter mundane life. Because there likely could be other beings who are kindly inclined to the babies and also to emphasize the respect and thanks to the Spirits and ancestors invited, additional non-specific offerings are given and, if nothing untoward happens, the Outsiders truce offering is poured out.

- - - - - - - - - - ~ - - - - - - - - - -

Closing the Gate

Keeper of Sacred Space:
Thank you, Great Bile!
Flourish still in all the worlds,
Stand ever tall, and every day,
Your protective leaves unfurl.

We love you, you love us,
Between us is the bond of trust.

Gatekeeper:
With our purpose here fulfilled,
Now our gathering is stilled,
The fire gone, the Well dry,
Magic dwindles with a sigh.
All is as it was before,
Let the Gate be here no more!

Thanking the Earth Mother

All: From you all of us were birthed,
Thanks from us, our Mother Earth!

Loretta's Mama:
I sacrifice for all past gifts,
Known and unknown, great and less.
I do not want to give short shrift.
Or seem to show unthankfulness.

Wendell's Momma:
All those who listen, hear our voice,
Thank you for your kindly choice.

Both make additional offerings.

Rewarding the Outsiders

Wendell's Dad:
We are glad to have had no pranks,
And for this, here's a toast and thanks.

Pours out the Outdwellers' offering.

Closing the Rite

Gatekeeper:
Go now, children of the Earth, in peace and blessings. The rite is ended!

All:
Woo!

Sheena MacIsaac has been studying magic since the age of 12, has been involved with Druidry of various forms since the age of 18, and currently defines her "path" as complicated.

Rae Green lives in Ottawa with her lovely partners, her many children, cats, and a largish dog, and spends her summers trying to escape the city for the tranquility of the Knoll.

ELEMENTAL JOURNEYS

by Anat Thompson

AIR

Begin this meditation by seeing yourself drifting over the sea
Lightly lifting the water into waves
Pulling water up into yourself and then dissolving back into the ocean
See yourself passing through every living creature
The air shared by all
Blenny and grouper, ray and shark, diatom and whale
Then see yourself rising back up to the surface as a bubble
and as the ocean breathes, you are exhaled upon the shore

You float upwards to the sky
You are caught on the wind
and it takes you higher and higher
You sail over the shoreline and see dunes of sand below
You blow strongly through the palm trees and tall grasses
You see them bowing and bending under your touch
You hear the sounds of your passing
as you rustle the leaves and rattle the dry grass

Feel yourself blowing harder and harder
Swirling and swirling, carrying tons of sand in front of you
You are now the sand storm that scours the landscape
that chaffs the skin and stings the eyes of the weary traveler
Allow yourself to bury that foolish traveler

that did not listen to the warning of the wise Elders

Lay bare the ancient knowledge
so long hidden beneath the sands of time
As you release the forms from their casts
and, slowly, you see a wall
a corner
a step
a pillar
and an entrance to a dark and ancient temple

You breathe new life into this room that has passed into myth long ago
You circulate the dust, mold and decay
and you replenish the room with a new found energy
The drawings on the wall come to life with new colour
As you blow away the layers of time
they smile back to you
and tell you of their lives, accomplishments, their hopes and dreams

Take a moment to read what the pictures are saying
for they have much to tell
Names, dates, places, ideas and wisdom
Messages and truths from a time long ago

You turn and look towards a dark niche
As you approach a face begins to emerge
You reach out to touch its features
They instantly wipe clean to show a beautifully painted eye
and then another eye
a mouth
a nose
chin, throat, neck, hair, jewelry and clothing

An idol emerges and you wonder
What is this?
What does it mean?
Whom reveres it and why?
As you step back and take in the sacred space
you see a story being played out
Events from long ago but not all that different from today

The sun peeks in through a window
That has not seen sun for a thousand years

and you sense yourself warming up in the sun's rays
You leave this place and travel on

Now you become the warm gentle breeze
moving towards tilled lands and sweet smelling soils
You swirl and dance amongst the vegetation
carrying the scent of newly blooming fruit trees
into the towns and villages
Where your scent makes people smile and remember

You lift their singing voices to the heavens
and tangle yourself in the hair of maidens as they dance
You lift their skirts as they twirl
and blow the clothing dry on the line

Now become aware of the light waves that pass through you
You see clearly all the different colors
and you feel the pulsating energy of the different wave lengths
You become the red light
and are made hot by passion and raw life energy
Then you are a clear and relaxed orange
tingling with attraction and positive experience
The orange becomes the clear yellow of health and mental alertness
the pure gold of sun
From this comes a clear deep emerald green
the colour of fertility and prosperity
Which gradually becomes the sparkling azure blue
of intelligence and intuition
The blue deepens, like a January evening
into a pure violet of spiritual wisdom
Which rapidly turns into the royal purple of power
Now you are the rainbow with all the colours swirling around
and through you
Dissolving into a blaze of white light

Through this white light you are lifted up
and you become the golden energy
that all life must breathe in order to survive
See yourself flowing in and out of plants, grasses and trees
You carry the call of the toad to its mate in a bog
You are the breath of the ferret as it comes up from its burrow
You are the currents of air beneath the wings of the hawk in flight

Ride on the wings of the hawk as it journeys
over the fertile fields
over the desert sands
and over the dunes on the shore

As the hawk flies along the shoreline
you notice that the hawk is flying towards a beautiful lagoon
The hawk circles the bay
and you notice the palm trees
Swaying in the warm gentle breeze

You let go of the hawks back
You thank the hawk for your ride
and you see the hawk disappear into the setting sun
You know in your heart that you will meet the hawk again

As you continue to drift down towards the lagoon
it becomes a clear blue pool of light …

WATER

Now see yourself floating in that clear blue pool of light
As you float you slowly become aware
that the pool of light is beginning to ripple and flow around you
and you are being rocked back and forth, gently
and then after a little while, more vigorously

Let the waters of the pool wash over you
and its currents draw you down into its depths
As you sink, relax
Breathe normally, for you are in the element of love and protection
and nothing can harm you here

Now imagine that the pool you are in is connected to the ocean
as you float through the channel
The current is pulling you out towards the sea
as you rush out towards the sea you feel your body becoming more solid
Salt crystals are making your form more buoyant
As you rise to the surface of the water
you can taste the bitter brine on your lips
Floating and undulating in the tides actions
The sunlight penetrates your skin and you feel its warmth

Soon you are tossed onto the surface of this great sea
You look around but there is no land in sight
The waves are turning into large breakers
You feel the exhilaration of the pounding waves within your body
The waves are pounding to the rhythm of your heartbeat
Flow with it, rock back and forth on the waves
As you float upon this great sea of life
you watch the sun chase the moon through the sky
Until they disappear over the horizon
Time and time again, that endless chase that needs no winner

You notice that the horizon has an outline of trees now
and you can hear the surf crashing on a distant shore
Slowly the tide carries you towards that shore
As you reach the shore you gently lap at the sand
Every time you reach out to touch the shore
Your touch turns to a white foam
that bubbles and spreads out over the sand
You feel the dry sand drawing you in closer to dry land

You pass through sand, root, rock and soil
and emerge from the ground as a spring well
For centuries you have come to this well
You are visited by all for nourishment
and revered by those who are wise in your ways

You pour out into a small rock basin
and provide answers to those who gaze deeply into you with questions
Through the rippling of shadow and light
you speak and hope they will understand

Then ripples appear on your surface
Lightly at first, then more frequently
A bank of dark clouds rolls in overhead
and the water of the heavens join you

You feel within yourself the approaching storm
The sound of thunder moves through you and
You feel the wind trying to draw you up into itself
The wind scoops you up and you are carried upwards into the rolling clouds
You are borne farther inland, high in the air
Over a vast range of craggy mountains
The air is so cold that you feel your body becoming sharp intricate crystals

and falling silently down onto the slopes of the mountains

Feel the cold and solidness of this form of water
Be the winter storm that rushes up into the mountains
Filling the valleys with silent, gently falling snow

Now, imagine yourself lying quietly as a vast plateau of snow
You feel the incredible potential of the earth below you
Feeling the heat of the spring sun above you
you begin to melt
Soaking deeper and deeper into the earth
As you sink into the earth you awaken all the forces of life
The seeds, roots, insects and plants
And, you call to the animals from their winter homes

Feel yourself moving up the trunk of the tree and into its branches
Then into the leaves and buds
You feel the swelling of the buds as you push through them
Its leaves unfurl and its flowers bloom
bursting with elation at the newly arrived spring

Feel yourself evaporating off the surface of the leaves
as they breathe you into the air
Feel yourself pushing up through the centre of a flower to glisten at its tip
As you sit at the tip, you shine and twinkle under the sunlight

A bee comes along and laps you up and carries you off to its hive home.
Feel yourself coalescing into pure nectar
With warmth you become the pure goodness of honey
Food for Gods and mortals alike.
You dance on the tongues of lovers and then are released back into the air
in their hot sweet breath

As you rise up towards the heavens you see vast fields and plains
that stretch out in all directions
The movement of the wind draws you towards an unfamiliar warmth
As you draw closer to it, you notice a vast fire below you
The brush and shrubs are nothing but smoking sticks
and the earth is black and hot behind the roaring flames
You feel the earth calling to you
and you desire to unite with the scorched earth
as you land and kiss the earths pain
You sizzle and dissolve into its porous skin and ease away its heat

As you wash the earth clean
you carry away debris and nutrients released by the fire
and collect into a channel where you become a steady creek
Then a rapid brook
and then, surging with more and more power, a mighty river
and as you rush down through the channel
You stretch out onto the riverbank and deposit the rich burden of silt

You travel many leagues as this river
Past field, plain and forest
Through rock and earth
Back out to the ocean and into the pool

You have come back to the clear blue pool of light
from whence you began this journey
Knowing that this cycle of water circulation never ceases
You have completed this part of your journey
But your travels are not over yet
You begin again but this time as earth …

EARTH

Breathe deeply
Now imagine that with each breath that you exhale
you feel yourself sinking into the ground
As you sink deeper you feel like you are falling backwards into the earth
Falling, sinking, you feel heavier and heavier
The weight of the earth
the pressure of thousands of pounds of rock weighs heavy on you
Relax and breathe normally
You are heavier and more solid than all of that rock and earth

Take several moments to sink deeper into the earth
Feel the different layers of earth pass through your body
You pass slower through the more dense layers
and move more freely through the porous ones
See yourself stretching and reaching through the many layers of time
You reach a layer of quartz rock
and you see yourself reflected thousands of time over in its surfaces
Then you reach a layer of igneous rock
and you feel the sharp glass like edges scratch at you

as you sink past its volcanic layer

You Will yourself to sink deeper
and you discover a river of lava
You quickly get swept up in the current and
You find yourself being forced upwards
and finally erupt at the mouth of the volcano
In a fiery stream of lava and ash arching across the sky

You have become a molten river,
and you find yourself pouring down the side of the mountain
Causing the ground to scream and moan under your heat and weight
You melt and absorb everything in your path
The weight of the debris you pick up
and the cool air, starts to slow you down
Until you plunge yourself into the hissing sea
That has not welcomed your arrival
You have stretched out over vast tracks of land

Time passes, you are not sure how long
You find yourself exposed to the workings of weather and nature
You can feel the wind rubbing against you
You feel the cold and heat of the passing seasons
Working at you trying to break you apart

You feel the tiny prying fingers of the mosses and lichens
Reaching as far as they can down into you for your valuable nutrients
Still more time passes
and you feel more porous as the rain seeps into you
and the unrelenting roots reach into you for foundation and sustenance

Give yourself some time to feel
the soft carpeting of the fallen leaves and petals
and the rich smell of decay
As they break down and become food for other life forms

You feel hundreds upon hundreds of little marching feet
As ants and other insects explore your newly available sediment
You feel the light tread of a spiders elegant walk and
the talons of small birds as they pick and claw at your surface

You feel the warm pads of the feet of small mammals
as they tread over you looking for food

Feel their tiny sharp nails as they burrow into you for shelter
and feel their tiny rapid heartbeats reverberate through you while they sleep
While they sleep you give them comfort, warmth and shelter
At least for a few hours of their perilous lives

Feel the smoothness of the serpent's belly
as she glides over and through you
Seeking a nook to sleep away the passing of the mid-day sun

Feel the warmth of their living bodies
and feel the cold weight of their dead carcasses
Allow yourself to be that much needed medium,
that allows life to come full circle

Suddenly you feel a rumbling from within
It approaches you from underneath
and from all around you
You sense panic in the small animals
as they flee in all directions
A deep crack falls open
The earth below you starts to shift and sink
You slowly merge back into the depths
You are covered by tons of earth and rock
and feel comforted by the weight on your body
For you know that your body is made of this earth
You are one in the same
And, though you have traveled
and have taken on different forms
you never really left

Sink further now, back into the earth
Where it is dark and warm
Your journey is almost complete
The darkness that surrounds you is as black as a void …

FIRE

Just allow yourself to float in the blackness for several minutes.
You notice a point of flame
Dancing and circling around at a distance
Then you see the point of flame moving rapidly towards you
Feel its longing, its desire for union as it rushes towards you.
Then it and you meet and both collide and erupt in a tremendous flare

Now allow yourself to see a barren, rocky planet
See the flames spouting out of crevices
and mountains being heaved up with great gout of lava and fire
Hear the deafening sounds of creative and destructive forces
Heaving and shifting great mounds of earth

You see fire, you are that fire
The Creator, The Destroyer
You are the white fire that burns across black skies
Rock, earth and stone melt and coalesce at your feet

Feel the fires of creation,
See the gases forming huge clouds
Finally the rains appear in a sky filled with blackened clouds
Listen as the rain falls onto your scorched earth
The water hisses at you and sputters at the moment of contact
Soon the unrelenting rain pushes your creative fury
back into the bowels of the earth
As a crust forms above you, you retreat back into the earth
To emerge another time

As your creative furies circulate within this massive ball of earth
They build up, you are the hottest you have ever been
White, hot, so hot that you are no longer in the form of fire
but that of pure energy
You seek out any slight, any weakness in your suffocating cage
You emerge as an earthquake light through the quartz
You strike out and reach for the sky above
You are magnified with the energy of 10,000 horses you burst out
And force yourself outwards to finally stretch towards the heavens
For you will only be contained of your own Will

Soon you find yourself rising and escaping upwards
You travel, how or for how long you are not certain
and notice a great forest
High trees with a mass of impenetrable thorns
And decaying undergrowth
You notice a stirring within you now
The collision of warm and cool air masses that are charged and unsettled
Feel the dry autumn air and the heaviness of the approaching storm
A rumbling

and then you strike
You release a white sheet of charged ions
You strike again this time at the ground below
Become that flash of lightning that streaks down from the heavens
And you hit an old dead pine

Feel the heat of the blaze as it spreads rapidly
Setting all around it on fire
Soon you are a great conflagration
Swept by the wild winds generated by your own heat
Feeding on all the dead and dry vegetation
Eating everything in your path

Everything that can run flees in front of you
And you consume that which cannot escape
You are finally stopped at a broad river
All that can feed your appetite, does
And nothing is left behind but charred ashes
Your last flames flicker bravely as the rain begins to fall

You are not extinguished, you can never be
And you transform back into that familiar form of energy
and dissipate into the air

Your journey leads you to another source of energy
You notice a small controlled fire and you merge with it
Now imagine yourself as a hearth fire
Feel the kindly warmth you are giving out
See the children and the adults lean towards you for warmth
Allow yourself to be the warmth that comforts their bodies
The wholesome food that is being prepare from your tender heat
Hear the crackling of your flames

You bring together people and ideas
Those wiser amongst the people tell stories of your journeys
Stories of your powers, Destructive and Creative

Those who dare to communicate with you do so with unpredictable effects
You are gazed into for answers
You are summoned by many of your given names
You burn the sweet smelling incense and herbs that are offered to you
To those whom you chose to reveal yourself to
You dance, flicker and mesmerize them

and punish those who are careless
to take too many liberties with your presence

You are the fire that teach lessons and morals
You are the fire in the eyes of the demons that haunt us
You are the fire in the sacred fires that liberate us
You are the fire in the Underworld of the Egyptians
You are the fire in the hands of Greek and Roman gods
You are the fire that the Jewish God rains down upon the unbelievers
You are the fire from beginning of time
and you are the fire that will come on Judgment Day

You also present within every man and woman
You are the drive and tenacity behind the Will
You are the fire of anger
You are the passion and lust of lovers
and you are the burning love between mother, father and child
You are the music that touches our souls
You are the light that guides us
You are the different forms of energy that drives us

Now you find yourself in the center of a particle accelerator
You are being studied and harnessed
For the energy you give off is like the fury of 1,000 suns
You are in the midst of that black void
You have now come full circle
Through air, water earth and fire
Your journey is complete …

                        … but never really over

Anat Thompson is Het Set, Het Eset, Het Ynpu, mother, wife, Pagan,
scribe in the service of MAAT, oneiromancer (studier of dreams), dancer,
chantress, priestess and servant for the House of Eset and Set.

.

DREAMING AT THE RAVEN STAGE

by Paul Connolly-Hartmann

Not everyone sees the Raven Stage as one of the holy sites on the Raven's Knoll land. It is where we hold concerts and plays. It is very much a public space, but that does not mean it is any less sacred.

I do not get to attend many work weekends, thanks in part to lack of time, and in part to lack of transportation. Raven's Knoll is quiet on those rare opportunities when I can come and lend a hand. The stage was newly built when I got such an opportunity, and I camped near to it to be close to the fire come night time.

Much of the ritual of work weekends doesn't involve circles or formal hails to Gods and Ancestors. It is the physical work that raises energy, and that energy ties us to the land as much as any formal rite. For me, on that weekend, helping to get the roof finished was my ritual. Handing plywood and tar paper up the ladder was my input to the land, as I was not then an experienced carpenter nor roofer. I did not mind, as I am well suited to heavy lifting. The work left me tired, but elated. The image of the raven caught in my mind.

When night came, I enjoyed myself at the fire much as anyone else does. There was some wine, some songs, and eventually the night's chill crept in. Tired from my day's labours, I sought my meagre sleeping pad and the comfort of my cloak.

It was likely sometime after midnight when I thought that I was awake, and that my tent was gone. I was under the sky, naked and unmoving. Above me circled something that interrupted the starlight, a black shape coming closer. I tried to move, but could not.

The raven landed on my chest, and looked at me. It occurred to me that I should be afraid, but I was not. I felt no menace from the raven, larger than I had seen before and somehow blacker. I could not move, yet I felt no danger. Not even when the raven's beak and talons began to dig at my chest.

By now I was vaguely aware that I was dreaming, yet it was all very real and vivid to me. For hours afterward in the morning, it was difficult to pin down exactly what the difference was between wakefulness and sleep. I suppose in the dream I felt less pain than I should have. To be clear though, it did hurt.

The raven dug its way into my chest, and I could feel it tearing strips from my heart. It gripped the organ in its talons and ate it, chunk by chunk. When all of it was gone, the bird wiggled slightly to fit itself into the hole, and folded itself up in the cavity between my upper lungs where my heart had been. I was dead, until its wings began to beat.

Slowly, in my dream, life returned to me. I was no longer in any pain, and I could move again. I inspected the hole in my chest, and found that while it was still there, it was a clean slit right through my breastbone, and it was not bleeding. If I tugged it open just a little, I could see the raven resting where my heart had been, its wings pulsing to pump my blood. I did not feel injured in the slightest. I felt strong, whole, and calm.

I returned to Ottawa, where I was living at the time, and did not speak of my dream to many. Yet it is still with me. Sometimes, when I close my eyes, I can still feel the flutter of a raven in my chest.

Paul Connolly-Hartmann is a Heathen, hailing originally from Toronto and educated at the University of Ottawa. He walks a path between shamanic personal experience and written lore, pulled by heart and intellect both. Paul also flies with the Monkeys at the Kaleidoscope Gathering.

A WALK TO THE MEN'S CAIRN

by John "Whitesnake" Lapchak

I wake up in the morning to the sound of birds chirping and the gentle breeze blowing through the trees. I get out of my tent and smell the fresh air and make myself a coffee. I sit and enjoy my coffee and ponder about the people in my life and the people who have left this world for the next. I can picture their faces as they walk up or down the Yellow Brick Road and wave to me with a smile and a "How's it going?" I remember the times spent with them and the things we have brought to each other's lives, and now that they are gone, I will miss these things. It makes me feel like I have lost someone profound in my life and I can no longer help them with any and all problems that they might have. I know that they are gone but they are certainly not forgotten. So I pick up my staff and two bottles of beer, and I begin. I begin my journey to be with them once again. My journey to the Men's Cairn.[i]

I walk down the road in silence, politely nodding and waving to those I pass but I always remain silent. As I get closer and closer I can feel the energies coming from the Cairn and I can feel the presence of those I cannot see but want to talk to.

I leave the road and walk through the parking lot and then onto a small path that winds through the brush. I have many times seen my Spirit Guide (The Snake) as I walk down this path. I stop for a moment as do they. We share a few seconds, looking at one another and I know that they are silently telling me that I must go to the Cairn because there is something I must hear and/or something I must say. I have not seen snakes every single time I have walked to the Cairn but every time I do see a snake on my journey, they always leave me and head off in the direction of the Cairn. One time the snake I saw went to the Cairn with me. Was I guiding it to the Cairn or was it guiding me?

I walk past the archery field and into a short curved path. As I come around the left side of the poplar facing me I see it: the Men's Cairn.

I stop immediately, ground and centre myself, and then I approach. With my eyes closed I sit for a while (sometimes a long while) and remember the people who have stood here with me in the past. I can remember the way they looked and sometimes I can hear their voices. I eventually start to talk out loud and speak of the things I have on my mind. My thoughts, my questions, my problems, all of the types of things we ask our friends about when we need advice or just an ear. When I am done with my questions I again sit in silence and wait for their words of advice to come to me. Sometimes it comes right away and sometimes it comes later but I have noticed it always does come.

I then take one of the bottles of beer and offer it to my departed friends and I start to drink mine. Once I have finished my beer I thank them for their advice and friendship and I pick up my staff and the now empty beer bottles and I stand at the edge of the short curved path that stands next to the large poplar and I look at the Cairn with great reverence.

As I walk away, I feel like I have just spent time with good friends and loved ones. As if they were right there in front of me but I do know that I will not see them again until I leave this world.

My walk back to my tent was the same as the walk from my tent, a silent walk. When I get back to my tent my girlfriend asks me, "How was your walk?" and I reply by saying, "It was great, I ran into some old friends."

In reading this you may think of the Cairn as being a tomb of sorts, a place to go to speak with the dead but that is not the case. I have gone alone to speak with the dead but I have also with other people who are very much alive. We speak of our lives, of our ups and our downs, our problems, of the good times and the bad. We share with one another just as I share with the departed.

The Cairn is not a tomb, it is a place where all men can gather and be with one another and gain strength from each other. The Cairn is different for each and every man that visits it. To some it is a place of quiet contemplation. For some it is a place where men gather to be men amongst other men. To some it is a place that represents men and the men that built it. I am sure there are many, many more points of view from others that I have not mentioned, but there are three things I know for a fact. One, the Cairn is sacred in some way to all of the different men who visit it. Two, I know what the Cairn gives to me and it is nothing but good. Three, I am happy and proud that I am among the group of men that founded the Men's Cairn and laid down the first stones.

Endnote:

i. All people that identify as men are welcome at the Men's Cairn; it is one's socially-lived gender identity, not their current or former biological sex, that is of importance. It is taboo for women and girls to be at the Men's Cairn. Boys, before their manhood ritual or age of majority, may be at the Men's Cairn in the presence of a man. Babes-in-arms are welcome with their guardian.

John "Whitesnake" Lapchak is a Pagan from the Montreal area who lives with his love Elena Brown. He is a licensed master carpenter and general contractor by trade. He has practiced Wicca for 20+ years and is an avid drummer at drumming fires and drumming circles. He is one of the founding builders of the Men's Cairn at Ravens Knoll, and can often be found meditating there. He has led the Men's Cairn walk many times and will continue to do so as often as he can.

A DAY IN THE LIFE OF A KNOLLTEER

by Christina

Volunteering at Raven's Knoll has been a big part of my life over the last few years. It's an experience I hold very dear to my heart and I make it out to as many of the work weekends that I possibly can. I will now walk you through my magical experience as a Knollteer.

My arrival at Raven's Knoll is usually before dinner on Friday as I promptly leave the city life to head to the wilderness of the Knoll. I then quickly set up camp but honestly it is just my tent, chair, cooler, air mattress, and sleeping bag so it does not take a great deal of time. I like to keep it very simple for the work weekends and since there is a food plan there is less to worry about. Next, while the campground is quiet I visit the sacred sites and leave an offering. Soon the other volunteers and staff will arrive.

That evening we relax around the Hearth Fire enjoying stories, songs, drumming, and good company. The fire dances to the sound of people talking and laughing. During the rare times it has rained we enjoyed some games in the Rookery. My fondest memory was a sumbel ritual we had at the last work weekend of 2014. Learning and sharing with the fellow members of the community makes for a stronger bond similar to an extension of family.

The next morning I awake to the forest sounds of frogs, squirrels, ravens, king fishers, blue jays, and the roar of the golf cart and the Black Pearl (the Knoll's truck). The cool morning air fills my lungs with anticipation and excitement for the day's tasks. But first breakfast is needed to fuel the day's work to come.

Breakfast and lunch are followed by a meeting to discuss tasks needed to be done and teams are made up to focus on these. Then, off with the newly formed teams which are made up of new and well-seasoned volunteers. The campground tasks include debris pickup, helping with the food plan, maintenance, repairs, and much, much more. On special occasions there is a creation of a Sacred Space on a work weekend; each one I find rewarding in different ways. The progression of a project and building your community is important. As well, I have learned much about every Sacred Space and gained knowledge of different aspects of religion from the other volunteers and staff. The weekend always includes getting to know a diverse range of people in the community either on teams or enjoying delicious work weekend meals. The friendships and kinship you create last a lifetime. I enjoy learning from new volunteers what drew them to the land.

One of the most important experiences to me was clearing the trees from the Spiral after Crazy Dave created it. It took several weekends of hauling trees and branches from the interior with a great team. The end result is my deeper connection with the Spiral and the forest surrounding it. Occasionally you will have a wild turkey briefly accompany you while you walk the path to the stangs.

For me it has been a long road of personal growth with openly accepting my religion and putting myself in the public eye. I have always been the quiet person in the corner and the Knoll has shown me I have a voice. This personal growth has been challenging but I have a family at the Knoll that has helped me. The time at Raven's Knoll has helped develop and put my skills to good use, while helping to create new ones. The feeling that I have contributed to building a place for our community to call home is priceless. Volunteering helps you build a community and your voice can be heard. Ideas can grow and be implemented. It is a wonderful process.

Not to mention the health benefits of picking up sticks!

Christina has been part of the Pagan community in the Ottawa area for close to five years. She first discovered her path as a curious teenager with a thirst for understanding, then later broke through her shyness to meet folks in the community. The first festival she attended was the Kaleidoscope Gathering in 2010 at Raven's Knoll, where an instant connection was made to the land. In 2011, she volunteered at the Rabbit Hole (KG registration) and at various work weekends through the years. She was raised in a family that camped, hiked, canoed, gardened, and appreciated the outdoors. Avid in recycling and composting, she has developed an appreciation for our delicate environment. Since 2009 she has been writing articles for her blog called "Small steps to help the environment."

A HERO'S THIRD GENDER RITUAL

by Jacky

I arrive at the Birch Grove having a vague idea of what will be involved in this year's Third Gender Ritual. The ritual leader is a friend of mine, after all. And I did have a say in the general "vibe" we were going for this year. But as usual, I am skeptical and don't think I will get into the headspace, and so a lot of what had been said about the rite got lost in the part of my brain where things go when I'm not sure what to do with them.

After some preamble, the main leader invites us to find a spot in the Birch Grove–our very own spot where we get to stay for most of the ritual. This is promising. It's much easier for me to get into a headspace by myself than with a crowd. In a crowd, I absorb too much of other people's energies. In my own bubble, I can focus on my own.

Our first task is to focus on our female hero. That's easy! A life sized figure of Xena: Warrior Princess appears in my mind's eye. Full leather gear, sword in hand, chakram at the waist, tall boots, and the usual sad/lonely/passionate/determined gaze. What can I learn from Xena? What feeds my so-called "female" self–so-called, because I don't give much cred to our sick society's gender essentialism–and drives the warrior in me? It doesn't actually wind up having much to do with gender in the end. After gazing off into the distance for a time, she looks me in the eye and says: "Remember who you're doing it for." A simple request to not make the same mistakes she has made. Don't get so caught up in "the struggle" that you forget that you are part of this world too. Human too. And that a struggle is most successful as a team or community effort. You can't do it alone. Take your time. Participate in people's healing. Let them participate in yours. Be with people. Let them be with you. Know them. Let them know you. Trust them. Let them trust you. Remember who you're doing it for–and remember what they are doing for you. That you are doing it together.

She leaves in time for me to hear that we are to focus on our male hero. Also easy. When I was a young'un, I wanted to be Robin Hood. And he also appears in my mind's eye. Also life sized, but not human! My Robin, of course, was Disney's version–an anthropomorphic fox! Green-clad, feathered cap, casually-held bow and arrow. And what can I learn from Robin? What feeds my "male" self (see above disclaimer) and inspires the nurturer in me? And again, gender is irrelevant. He chuckles mischievously and…just winks, grins and turns away. I understand what he is telling me. "Keep laughing." Be a trickster. Know when not to be a trickster. Always be ready with a smile. Smile at the people you love. Smile at the people you don't know. Smile at the people you can't stand. Make them laugh. Help keep them merry. There is a great value in entertainment. Escapism is not just for the weak. But humour and a mischievous disposition can't hide depth, passion, and caring. The less afraid you are to look like a fool, the more people will respect you.

He's gone in time for me to hear that we are to focus on our Third Gender hero. Huh? What heroes do I have that are Third Gender? Are there any? What counts as a hero? I come face to face with Jennifer Miller: Bearded Lady, Circus entertainer, juggler, and fire-eater. A real life person, not a fictional character. Someone alive. She identifies as a woman, but has lived with a beard for most of her adult life and so is one perfect model, for me, of living between the binary genders. It appears that I'm interrupting her in the middle of a juggling practice. She seems annoyed. I don't blame her. If someone visualized me so strongly that I was forced into communication with them when I was concentrating on something important, I'd be quite frustrated. I'm not sure what to say in the face of her impatient and inquiring look. So I just say that I admire her strength. Her courage to live as she is with no apologies. I wish I could do the same. I am sick of binding my breasts so that I can "pass" as a person with a binary gender but I don't have the courage to live full-time as "in-between". I don't feel I have the energy. She shrugs and tells me that she just does it. There comes a time when you just do it. When your own comfort with yourself becomes more important than avoiding the looks and the giggles. More important even than avoiding the possible violence. "But you already know that–you didn't need me to tell you." I cry, because she's right. Am I not the one who once said: "Sometimes being an activist simply means being yourself"? As with the other two heroes, the message really does have little to do with gender. But it has everything to do with knowing oneself.

The ritual is over. I slowly come back to the Birch Grove. Looking around, I see that others have had moving experiences. Some people look pensive. Some look giddy. Some are in tears. Some are hugging. I keep most of my energies to myself, still trying to sort them out. But I still feel connected to the others who shared this space.

I feel rooted and content in the Birch Grove with its perfect level of containment: circular without being closed off. Surrounded by graceful but sturdy trees, the circle of sand supports us while absorbing our words, thoughts, energies. Not just one thing, this Birch Grove–perfect for the annual Third Gender ritual where we encourage each other to go beyond the binary, even if just for the duration of the ritual. Where we support each other in exploring other ways of being and knowing. Where anyone can stick their toe, or more, into the embodiment of a gender other than the one they grew up in so that they can better know and love themselves.

The ritual leader closes the ritual. I leave the Birch Grove not having told anyone about my experiences. That will come. For now, I take the energy with me back to camp and, later on, back home and meditate on the visions, knowledge, and energy that were shared between humans and others in the Birch Grove that day.

Jacky with a Y is a Two-Spirit mixed-heritage animist, anthropologist, teacher, parent, activist and underground stage performer living in Montreal. He is making his way to the Red Road, observes an eclectic set of pre-Christian European traditions, and is influenced by early Gnosticism. He is allergic to dogmatism and oppression. Il parle français aussi! You can read some other ramblings of his at http://jackywithay.wordpress.com.

THE PET CEMETERY

by Maryanne Pearce

When we bought Raven's Knoll, I had been doing dog rescue for about a year. I specialize in Great Pyrenees dogs, but mutts and cats have been thrown into the mix too. One of the sad realities about not only animal rescue but pet ownership in general is that pets die and your heart breaks.

The need for a pet cemetery arose in our first camping season, 2010. A cat we had adopted from a friend of mine in 1996 had passed away. Our first long weekend was our first event, the Midgard Festival. We had brought Simon (Paul Simon Pearce-Lawrence) up to be buried that weekend.

I had arrived early on the Friday, alone. Brendan "the Handy" Roche, our land manager, was there but sleeping as he worked nights. The first campers for Midgard, Mandy and Jeff Helmes, had arrived an hour before I had but no one came to the door so they left and returned shortly after I got there. I greeted them in the house, chatting with them and welcoming to the Knoll. I had the feeling I knew the woman but we could not place it. After they had driven down to set up camp, I thought to myself I should ask my sister if she knew a Mandy who had lived in Kitchener. As soon as this passed through my mind, it all came together.

I grabbed my keys and raced below. I jumped out, van door left wide open and ran across the grass. Mandy was running towards me. "Do you know who you are?" I shouted at her. She was grinning and nodding. "You are Simon's first mommy!"

It was 12 years since we last had a visit from Mandy. Much had changed for both us and it was just so unexpected a reunion that we had not put the pieces together. Mandy and Jeff had never been to a Pagan event before; we had not crossed paths since Mandy had left for B.C. And here she was: the woman who had asked me to watch her cat for a few days, 14 years ago.

Here, at the Knoll, for his funeral. Mandy and I placed Simon, along with a cup of our dog Kira's ashes, into the ground. The first inhabitant of what would grow into our pet cemetery. Simon, in his death, reunited his human mothers. It was bittersweet; tears and laughter.

Many people have helped with this endeavour. Kadri Weiler, Brenda Lee and Ckw created the archway. Jacqueline Thomas mapped the interred. Brendan and Lugh Sulian did the mowing and most of the digging for new placements. In 2014, Jesse Wiegand from Alberta finished the hole Kevin had started for our beloved Boudica–the water level was too high to bury a huge dog. During a heat wave, Jesse dug down another three feet so we could inter Boudica.

Each pet has a wooden placard with their name which I order from a Pagan artisan. We do not charge for interments, although a few people have kindly provided donations. We have dogs, cats, ferrets, birds and a chipmunk within the borders. For those who have no ashes or body to inter, the placard is for the archway.

Loving and caring for animals is part of my spiritual path. That is true for many others among us. The spirits of those who have left us remain free to wander and visit, just as I visit them all. Heartbreak cannot be avoided when we love, animal or human. All must pass beyond the veil. For those animals beloved of our community, a home exists among the trees for their earthy remains while their spirits run in Summerland. In my mind, Summerland looks a lot like the Knoll.

Maryanne Pearce, also known as MA, is one of the Stewards of Raven's Knoll and a co-organizer of the Kaleidoscope Gathering. She holds a doctorate in law, focusing on missing and murdered vulnerable women. Her Master's thesis in Anthropology focused on the Canadian Pagan community. MA is in charge of all the paper involved with RK and KG. She lives in Ottawa with her husband Austin Lawrence, her two adult children Kadri Rainne and Joven Wolf, and various four legged friends.

THE STAG KING

by Jordan Phoenix

The Stag King ritual is a modern rite based on traditional elements, combining them to make them more fitting for our present age. By adopting ritual elements from a variety of spiritual paths ranging from age-old tribal ceremonies to contemporary Heathen and Pagan rites, and fusing them with contests of strength, martial prowess, and will, assembled from time-honored trials such as Highland games, Strong Man competitions, Lumberjack championships and the Olympic games, the Stag King ritual is a unique ritual and competition unlike any other.

The Stag King ritual, while having achieved a great deal of prominence over the years of its running, had an exceptionally unassuming beginning. Loki, a member of the Ontario Pagan community,[i] was following his spiritual path and seeking wisdom, and in his travels he witnessed a Beltane ritual in British Columbia that was named the Stag King. This contest, a combination of physicality and spirituality intrigued him, and stayed with him; years later circumstances would bring this ritual back to Ontario.

During the Kaleidoscope Gathering festival it is tradition that a men's ritual and a women's ritual are held to explore and glorify the divinity in each of the binary genders. It occurred that during the eleventh year of the festival that the men's ritual was to be cancelled after the organizer fell ill, and it would be a year that no men's ritual would occur. This fact did not sit well with some people and so one person took it upon himself to improvise a ritual on the spot from his recollections of the rite he witnessed years ago; the tools for the ritual were provided by the natural surroundings, and the framework for the event was planned with advice of selected community elders. Hastily, rudimentary spears were gathered from saplings and fallen limbs, a ring was cleared on sandy ground to allow for safe combat and the men of the folk of the festival were invited to join the ritual by criers who ran the length and breadth of the festival grounds. From this small nucleus of assembled men, one was able enough to prove himself the worthiest of his fellows and be crowned the Stag King.

The following year, no Stag King ritual was held as the customary men's ritual occurred without issue. The year following that, the Kaleidoscope Gathering festival went on hiatus as the location of the event had to be changed. In the first year of the festival held at Whispering Pines, again the men's ritual was cancelled suddenly and again Loki was in attendance along with the first and still-reigning Stag King. These two, along with a chosen few community Elders, arranged to hold the rite of the Stag King. Once again rough tools were gathered, a ritual space and field of combat were cleared and criers were sent across the festival grounds to announce the event. The men of the folk then assembled, competed, and hours later the soon-to-be King faced the old King, needing to first "slay" him in ritual combat. This fight was executed before the cheering people of the festival to attest to the worth of the new King and to prove that the old King had indeed been deposed, and made incapable of ever holding that station again.

While the public spectacle of the Stag King ritual is impressive and the trials which are organized away from public eyes are both grueling and satisfying for the competitors, the ritual itself has deep roots that reach into some of humanity's most ancient traditions. The Stag King ritual where each new King of the folk is selected is based on the historical figure of the Sacral King, the notion of which has prehistoric origins and can be found worldwide. Using a variety of ancient texts, contemporary scholars have defined a Sacral King as "one who is marked off from his fellow men by an aura of specialness which has its origins in more or less direct associations with the supernatural".[ii] In Western Europe during the beginning of the Middle Ages, among the Pagan Irish, kings were viewed as representatives of the entirety of their peoples, and had not only to reflect exceptional qualities, but also to fulfill certain duties, corresponding to each of the divisions of their society.[iii]

The Sacral King simultaneously represented and transcended the social hierarchy, which provided for a role as the ideal intermediary between the divine and human realms, expressed through participation in communal ritual. As the embodiment of society, the King was the perfect representative of the totality of society, thus when he performed ritual it was as if all his subjects were involved in that activity, greatly amplifying its efficacy. Kings, without being priests, could act as interlocutors connecting those they ruled with the Gods themselves.

The Pagan kings of the Irish, Germans, and Scandinavians were more often than not viewed as representing the moral and domestic ideals of their culture, and personifying the fate of their people. Through their communion with the divine the Sacral Kings were duty-bound to assure the good fortune of those they ruled. The King was expected to rule justly, bringing prosperity to his realm by means of "the sovereign's truth." Through "the sovereign's truth" came an abundance of grain in the fields, fruit on the trees, milk from cattle, and fish in the rivers; internal peace was maintained, and victory over enemies granted; the well-being of sages and the continuity of the various arts was assured. However, if the King ruled unjustly, signs would appear that his land would fall to ruin through "the sovereign's falsehood"; fruit would rot, grain would be scarce, milk-cows would go dry, famine would occur; the King would suffer defeat in battle, and the priesthood would be troubled.[iv]

To escape the dire fate of a false sovereign, the people would often attempt to placate the divines by deposing the False King in hopes of appeasing the Gods through this act of bloodless sacrifice; though by some accounts this sacrifice could and often would be accomplished by ritually taking the old King's life and installing a new and more suitable King to rule.[v]

To avoid appointing an unsuitable or "false sovereign," the ritual of the Stag King bases the awarding of the role not on any inherited rights or balloted voting, but rather places the success or failure of the hopeful King in their own hands and at the will of the Divines. The ritual of the Stag King is held annually and calls upon the men of the folk to stand up and be tested; he that proves himself the best becomes our Sacral King to reign, conferring upon the folk his vitality and good fortune. After his year has passed and the ritual has been held again, a new King will be crowned and the old King must be "slain" so that the old King may never grow complacent and the folk will always be rewarded with a new King full of fresh vigor and his own unique gifts to bestow upon the folk.

This willing acceptance of the Stag King to act as a sacrifice for the greater good mirrors much of the folklore surrounding the stag, a creature seen legendarily as the protector of the land who willingly lays down its life to provide for those that seek to consume it. The nature of the stag is to be hunted; it is his agreed role and, while he may act as lord of the forest, it is his destiny to die.

The myths and lore surrounding the stag run across the world from the mythic reindeer of ancient Lapland, all the way back to the earliest history from Sumerian of Dara-Mah "The Great Stag."[vi] This ancient figure is suspected by modern scholars to have been a fertility and/or protector God of nature. The masculine God-figure's identification with the stag is significant, as the stag was not a particularly important animal to very many deities and religions in the other historic Indo-European pantheons. Bears, boars, ravens, and many other animals are well represented as the totemic animals of Gods and Goddesses across the Indo-European spectrum.

However, in Classical times the stag was of paramount importance to the Scythians and other peoples across the Eurasian steppes.

The stag was one of the favorite motifs of the Neolithic Proto-Indo-European peoples, and so its history as a figure of veneration amongst the Indo-European peoples is very ancient. As a wild and majestic animal, we should not doubt that the genesis of this deity's veneration began before even the Neolithic period. It is thought that the "Stag God" originated in the steppes, and that he was brought to the crossroad of Anatolia, the historical boundary where Asia and Europe met, by the early Indo-Iranian peoples.

One of the widest known examples of a "Stag God" in the Western world is Cernunnos, "the Horned One," who is classically depicted with ram horns or antlers. His most famous depiction being that on the Gundestrap cauldron, where he is the main figure and is shown as having a most extravagant set of antlers. The development of Cernunnos in Celtic religion may have been early or he may have been adopted after the eighth century BCE when Scytho-Cimmerian elements from the Eurasian steppes entered central Europe.[vii]

The symbol and reverence of the stag (apart from the Stag God) amongst the Anglo-Saxons is a tradition that is very likely to be rooted in the most ancient of Germanic culture and religion. In England we know such reverence of stags was already a custom as a letter to Pope Gregory the Great from Saint Augustine of Canterbury (who had been sent to convert the Anglo-Saxons to Christianity) condemns the Pagan practice of "dressing up like a horse or stag."[viii] Like so many of the other animal symbols connected to the Anglo-Saxons, we only have to look at the Sutton Hoo ship burial for evidence. Within the burial was found a spectacular scepter that was crowned with an exquisite figure of a stag. For the person who carried it, the scepter no doubt symbolized their power and high status. And it could be that amongst the Heathens the stag was regarded as the most noble and proud of animals, and would therefore be a most appropriate symbol of a King and his leadership. Strong evidence pointing to the use of stag images in sacred rites and the worship of stags, can be found in writings of scholars who recorded these acts of worship performed by the Pagans of the British Isles during the early Middle Ages.[ix]

One reason stags were venerated was that they were seen as a source of hidden knowledge. The quest for wisdom is found frequently in mythology surrounding stags; a common story among various ancient cultures is that deer are the animal that provides humankind the secret knowledge of how to hunt. In return, humankind promises not to abuse this gift and never to hunt to excess, or waste the flesh or hide of the animals they do kill.[x] From the Sámi,[xi] and other tribes across the globe whose lives are reliant upon deer, we can understand how central the knowledge of successful hunting and the understanding of how to utilize the whole of the carcass was. When you, your family and your entire tribe's clothing, diet, tools and thus survival are reliant on a single animal then they become symbolic of life. The knowledge required to hunt them becomes irrevocably tied up with the knowledge required for life. Thus, the stag and the doe have become an ingrained mythic symbol in many societies. Furthermore, the stag is seen as a strong image of renewal, not merely because the herds of deer replenish year after year, but in particular the antlers of the stag are shed and re-grown every year, and in this way the stag itself comes to symbolize rejuvenation and rebirth. Antlers are also a potent symbol, both for virility and fertility, but also as an allegory for the forest itself: the antlers being seen as the broad limbs of the tree of life, a fitting image for the creature often called the Lord of the Forest.

We can see how the figure of the Stag King strives to encapsulate both the ancient mythology of the stag who was viewed as either an aspect of the masculine god figure or a semi mythical creature that acted as an envoy between the physical and spiritual planes, and the long standing tradition of the Sacral King who provides for his people by giving of himself and his own divinely conferred gifts. The King who stands for nobility, honour and a strong commitment to the protection of his people, and the Stag who acts as an interlocutor between mortals and their Gods, while also sharing sacred wisdom and appearing as the living embodiment of nature and the forest itself.

So grew an annual trial that would become larger and more significant year by year as the men of the folk were challenged bodily, mentally, and spiritually. While the early years' trials focused principally on the physical aspects of strength, endurance, agility, and precision; even in those early contests there was an understanding among the judges of the competition that physical prowess would not be the only aspect of the competitors that they would evaluate. At all times the men were scrutinized for their valor, comradeship, and nearly ineffable quality of "heart" that is difficult to define, but obvious to see in action. An offered hand to a fallen competitor and an enthusiastic hug between those that had been fiercely wrestling moments earlier; words of encouragement or advice freely given to those that oppose your goal of becoming the Stag King; these are the traits looked for by those presiding over the ritual, as these qualities are what make a man worthy of the mantle "Stag King."

Each year as the ritual has grown it has changed, in part to keep those that have participated in the past from having too much knowledge about the trials to come, and in part to reflect the will and desires of the King who still reigns. Before the old King will pass the mantle and allow himself to be "slain" by his successor, it was sensible that he deem the new King worthy and therefore test him in a manner which he saw fitting. Various Stag Kings have added new tests of strength, trials of wit and creativity, as well as spiritual components that dare the challengers to look within and contend with what they find inside. And at the end of each ritual, a new King is named, an old King is slain, and the prosperity of the people ensured. The Stag King is the leader of the folk, one who has demonstrated his worthiness to reign through numerous trials both physical and mental. Strength, agility, creativity, and character are the virtues each man must call upon to rise to the challenge and become King of the folk.

Hail the Stag King.

The following is a list of the men who have
served their community as the Stag King.

2000 - Douglas Thew
2001 - No rite
2002 - No rite
2003 - Cliff Hope
2004 - Blair Arch
2005 - Jordan Phoenix
2006 - Logan Leroux
2007 - Patrick Naughton
2008 - Tyler Mulligan
2009 - Austin (Auz) Lawrence
2010 - Greg Wiebe
2011 - Adam Simpson
2012 - Jean Sébastien Daunais
2013 - Greg Currie
2014 - John (Hobbes) Hickey
2015 - Prudent Wolf
2016 - Zach Imrie

- - - - - - - - - - ~ - - - - - - - - - -

Endnotes:

i. Loki [Craft name]
ii. McTurk, Rory. (1974) *Sacral Kingship in Ancient Scandinavia. A review of some recent writings*. Viking Society for Northern Research Saga Book Vol XIX, University College London
iii. Bray, Daniel, (1997) *Sacral Elements of Irish Kingship*, in Carole M. Cusack and Peter Oldmeadow (eds.), *This Immense Panorama: Studies in Honour of*

Eric John Sharpe, School of Studies in Religion University of Sydney; online at escholarship.usyd.edu.au/journals/index.php/SSR/article/viewFile/660/6404

iv.   Audacht Morainn from Koch, John T., and John Carey (eds.), *The Celtic Heroic Age*. Literary sources for ancient Celtic Europe and early Ireland & Wales, Aberystwyth: Celtic Studies Publications, 2003.

v.   Melanie Giles (2009). Iron Age bog bodies of north-western Europe. Representing the dead. *Archaeological Dialogues*, 16

vi.   Ida, Bobula. The Great Stag: A Sumerian Divinity and its Affiliation. University of Buenos Aires, 1953.

vii. Macculloch, J.A. (1911) *The Religion of the Ancient Celts*.

viii. Jones, Putnam Fennell (1928). The Gregorian Mission and English Education. *Speculum*, 3.

ix.   *The Prose Works* by Aldhelm; Michael Lapidge; Michael Herren (Translators) Boydel & Brewer (2009)

x.   Swan, James A. *The Sacred Art of Hunting: Myths, Legends, and the Modern Mythos*. Willow Creek (2000)

xi.   The Sámi people are the indigenous people of northern Europe inhabiting Sápmi, which today encompasses parts of northern Sweden, Norway, Finland and the Kola Peninsula of Russia.

Jordan Phoenix is known in the Pagan community for his mead making skill and (almost) excessive height. He has been attending and volunteering at various Pagan events for over 20 years. Jordan is largely a solo practitioner of Paganism. He finds his greatest connection to his spirituality in the solitude of hunting. Jordan is a former Stag King of the Kaleidoscope Gathering.

THE TRIALS OF ARTEMIS:
COMMUNITY, RITUAL, AND THE LAND

by Kimberly Ross

The Trials of Artemis is a ritual event which was started at Kaleidoscope Gathering in its first year at Raven's Knoll in 2010. In it, any women of the community who wish to participate take up a series of challenges in order to determine who amongst the candidates will carry the title of Huntress for the following year, the symbolic protector and provider of the community.

Since ritual is generally considered the domain of religion or spirituality, particularly in the context of land such as Raven's Knoll, I also wish to share my own perspective on its importance. As someone who does not have faith-based beliefs, I feel it is important to address why I became involved with the Pagan community and many of its rituals.

The Importance of Ritual, Community and the Land

I have always been a humanist, rather than a spiritualist or believer, and many have asked what I see in a spiritual community or why I participate in, or organize, rituals in the Pagan community. I have also been a strong supporter for Pagan-owned land within my chosen community, and some have been puzzled by that.

My answer to these questions begins with my studies of anthropology, and that I see community as one of the most important things people need to have. A place where a community can build their dreams, can assemble without restriction, and which can be modified to fit the needs of that community, is particularly beneficial. I feel that dedicated land is especially important for Pagan communities, who are oriented to nature, and for those of us who share a sense of wonder in the natural world, if not the same spirituality. Raven's Knoll fulfills that need for the community, and I am proud to be a part of forging some of the new traditions that make it a unique space.

In that light, for a community to be cohesive and functional, few things are more important than ritual. It fosters bonding between members of the community, aids individuals in their journeys of personal growth, and contributes to a united sense of purpose. It reassures people that they are not alone, that they share a commonality with others. It helps to ease the pain and discomfort of change or loss. It helps us feel a sense of unity and accomplish tasks that none of us could achieve alone. It can help us resolve problems, or bring concerns to light. It can help us to heal, to end a phase of our life, or to begin a new chapter.

Understand that ritual is a broad term to me, and encompasses many habits and events, not necessarily spiritual in nature. A morning cup of tea or an established way of ending the day is a ritual. An event at a particular time and place is an ritual. For me, these rituals include a weekly meeting with fellow writers, a bi-weekly game with friends, a monthly full moon get-together, Christmas dinner with my family, and attending Kaleidoscope Gathering each year. A more specific attendance ritual for me is that every time I go to Raven's Knoll, I visit the bonfire space.

Any gathering or action for a specific reason, be it formal or informal, ceremonial or casual, is a ritual. A sumbel in the Heathen tradition is less formalized, while an opening ritual for a festival or a coming-of-age ceremony is more formally structured, according to its tradition, but they are all ideally structured to serve their purpose.

For me, ceremonial ritual is about purpose; it drives us and motivates us. That purpose may be as simple as bringing order and inclusion to the members of the community, or as complex as sharing grief over loss or building strength to overcome obstacles. The formal elements of ritual have always been less important to me, as long as the ritual structure inspires the participants' thoughts and brings them together.

There are a few occasions which stand out in my mind as a illustrations of community and the importance of ritual within it. One of these occurred just after a sumbel I had attended. It came up in conversation with a few of the other participants that I was not spiritual, and one of my friends asked politely why I attended sumbels if that was the case. My reply was that a sumbel was one of the best community building rituals I had ever come across, and that was why it held value for me. She and the few others there accepted my perspective in stride, recognizing that our motivations were much the same, despite our differences. This is one of the many reasons why I regard the Pagan community as my community, despite the absence of spirituality on my part.

I first began to understand the importance of formal rituals many years ago, though. An accident occurred one night around the bonfire at a festival, and people were injured. Throughout the next day, I heard people not only discussing it, but dwelling on the negative feelings this had caused to be associated with the bonfire itself. I was driven to remind people that the bonfire was a place of celebration and love. I didn't want to make people forget about the injuries, or that fire must be respected and well-tended, only that there was still happiness and warmth to be found there, that it did not have to be tainted by unhappy events.

A few friends helped me cobble together a cleansing ritual which we performed at dusk. As ceremonial rituals went, it was quite informal. The purpose of the ritual was to cleanse the space of fear and negative thoughts in the minds of the festival participants. It was impromptu, so not many people were there, and only a few more drifted in as we proceeded. We waved them in as we went, and finished with a happy-toned, uplifting chant about fire.

As the bulk of the festival participants showed up, the mood was tentative, but as word spread of the cleansing ritual that had been performed, the mood improved. Between the ritual and people's natural resiliency to misfortune, the night continued in the spirit it was intended to. Whether one believes in the spiritual power of ritual or not, the act of drawing people's attention to a common goal, even just the knowledge that it had been done, brought members of the community into a common purpose and intent, to reaffirm the celebratory nature of the space.

I have run or helped to organize many other rituals and events since then, all of which have been aimed at contributing to the community as a whole. Many have focused more on intent than formal elements, and some have not been ritualistic at all except in their aspect of traditional repetition. Whether it is the Trials of Artemis, the Women's Warrior Circle, a yearly discussion of anthropological topics relating to the theme of the Kaleidoscope Gathering, or a new tradition of a fire keeper's weekend at Raven's Knoll, these all have an aspect of ritual to me. They all bring people together with the goal of adding positively to the community as a whole in one way or another. They are all events which are held in a certain time and place, and they all call Raven's Knoll home.

The symbolic importance of Raven's Knoll to the community that populates it is valuable even to those of us who hold no beliefs. It is about community, and a place in which we can come together to support and celebrate each other. It is a place where traditions can be formed with a sense of permanence and collective identity, where rituals take on greater meaning because of the dedicated purpose of the land.

How the Trials of Artemis Began

For the Trials of Artemis, we wanted to create something for a specific purpose: a ritual, but not one bound to habit, nor one that was rigidly formalized. Even the name was carefully chosen, after much deliberation, to convey that this was a challenge, but also an acknowledgement of prowess and skill. We wanted to structure a space where women could explore aspects of themselves that are often neglected. Not the nurturing, domestic, craft-oriented, sensitive aspects, but the fiercely resolute, innovative, clever, strong, and powerful aspects.

It began as a conversation between my good friend Elaine and I, but it took some years before we were able to fully form the details of what was needed, and set to doing it. Elaine came up with many of the ideas for the first set of challenges, and between the two of us we ironed everything out to run almost smoothly. The first year it happened was the first year that the Kaleidoscope Gathering took place at Raven's Knoll, which seemed an appropriate time and place for a new tradition to be born. It almost immediately took on a life of its own, and we knew that we had gotten the right idea.

I don't know about Elaine, who was only there for the first year, but from the time I took over the organizing of it, to the time I handed it off to the Huntresses and Elders of the community, I have fielded many questions, comments, and critiques about the Trials. Foremost amongst these was the assumption that it was merely the women's equivalent of the Stag King Competition. While it does fulfill a similar niche for its participants and the community as a whole, the Trials have their own distinct philosophy.

The Trials of Artemis reflect a rejection of socially accepted gender roles, as well as celebrating qualities that typically are less encouraged for women. The challenges are aimed partly at countering stereotypes, with an emphasis on celebrating a whole and complete woman, who can unselfconsciously relate her abilities and accomplishments, who can lead, protect, provide for, and understand her wider community. It is based on modern principles of equality, past egalitarian ideologies, and on the accomplishments of historical women who are often neglected in history texts. Drawing on the past for inspiration is an important part of this ritual for me, as part and parcel of the desire to inspire people in the future with our actions.

There is a wealth of historical and archaeological information to draw on as far as excellent women role-models are concerned, from pre-historic times right up to the modern day. Some are well known, such as Boudicca, who led her people against the Romans, or the politically powerful Queens of medieval Spain, who shaped the course of their nation. Hatshepsut of

Egypt, and many powerful matriarchs of influential Italian families, such as the Borgias, are also familiar names. Less well-known are the women warriors and leaders whose graves have been discovered across the breadth of Northern Europe and Eurasia. Many of them were assumed to be male based on the items found with them, until further analysis was performed.

Many less well-known women recorded by history were leaders of their people in times of war as well as peace. In the first century, Veleda was a leader of the Rhineland tribe of the Bructeri. She led in both the political and spiritual arenas, serving as an arbiter during negotiations between Rome and Cologne and acting as a prophetess for her tribe. The Roman writer Tacitus underscored the connection between her roles in military and religious life when he described her as "a maiden of the tribe of the Bructeri, who possessed extensive dominion; for by ancient usage the Germans attributed to many of their women prophetic powers and, as the superstition grew in strength, even actual divinity. The authority of Veleda was then at its height, because she had foretold the success of the Germans and the destruction of the legions."

Respected and powerful women are also reflected as deities or important figures in the mythologies of many cultures: Isis, Kali, Athena, Astarte, Frigga, the Fates, the Valkyries, the Morrigan, and of course, Diana or Artemis.

Artemis, of the Greek pantheon, is a Goddess of the hunt, the wilderness, the mistress of animals, and the protector of girls and women. She is depicted as a master of the bow, and a hunter of unparalleled skill, but also associated with childbirth. She was chosen as the namesake of the ritual because she embodies the idea that being a strong, fierce, independent hunter and being a caring protector are not incompatible roles. These are ideals to which all people can aspire, be they men or women.

Without wanting to really delve into gender politics too much, a small mention is unavoidable. Particularly for women in our society, strength, pride in accomplishment, and independence are qualities that are not valued often enough. One of the intents of this annual ritual is to explore and encourage these attributes, and it has not been without its obstacles. On several occasions, men in the community have offered unsolicited advice on how to conduct the ritual, where they would not have had it conformed to more conventional aspects of femininity.

While I realize the good intentions behind most of them, these people are often blind to the idea that women, even in this community, very much need to cultivate their own personal agency. One of the many purposes of this ritual is to do this as women, for women, without the need for aid or advisement of men. It is an expression of capability and autonomy in the face of wider social discrimination that we come together and demonstrate our prowess.

This sense of equality and independent authority is at the heart of the Trials. Even the name reflects the reality of overcoming assumptions and expectations. It hearkens back to legends and myths where the huntress was as respected as the hunter, and where the warrior woman needed no man's approval to be who she was.

The Trials of Artemis

The Trials are meant to choose the best among the community; she, who among many skilled and talented people, is chosen to be the symbolic representation of strength, resourcefulness, capability, truth, and wisdom for the community as a whole.

The challenges themselves vary widely, but are designed to determine certain qualities in the candidates. Some are individual trials, while others involve working with a group. Some are more competitive, with objective scoring, while some are judged more subjectively on the participant's actions or words, but the ultimate decision of who is to be the Huntress falls to the Elders of the community who oversee the ritual.

Some of the trials test for physical prowess and skill, such as running, archery, or throwing. Others seek out resourcefulness and innovation by crafting objects or hunting tools from the surrounding environment, finding symbolic items, or exploring ways to accomplish goals with few materials.

Cleverness and wisdom are also sought for by solving riddles, thinking creatively and overcoming physical obstacles through intelligence. Another set of trials cover personal confidence and the participant's ability to express themselves and their ideas well.

Throughout, the Elders observe for less measurable traits such as leadership, integrity, sense of community, and conviction. In the end, the title of Huntress may not go to the strongest or the fastest, but to the woman who is most capable and embodies the qualities that are needed in a protector, provider, and role-model for her people.

Though the Trials of Artemis consist mostly of the various challenges, a part of it is more ceremonial, serving to unite the would-be Huntresses in their shared experience, strength, and sense of community. Below is an example of one of the formal ritual portions used in the past for the Trials of Artemis. It does not emphasize any particular spiritual path, though it includes elements from several, in order to be as meaningful to every participant as possible.

We gather here to honour the memory
and the traditions of our Ancestors,
and the women who came before.

We come from Artemis, Diana: the mighty huntress.
We come from Boudicca, warrior queen,
from Sekhmet, the vengeful hunter,
and from the Valkyries of the North.

We keep alive the tradition of women who have been strong,
who have been wise, who have protected and provided for their people.
We do this to honour those who came before,
and to inspire those who will follow.
To the huntress of yesterday: hail!

From the past, to those who stand ready,
feel the spirit of the huntress flow through you.

We connect to the energies of the Earth,
that our roots grow deep,
that we stand fast in all weather,
that we have the strength of stone.

We connect to the energies of the air,
that we hear the voices of our people,
that we move like the wind,
that we speak the truth.

We connect to the energies of the water,
that we feel the pulse of our people,
that we know patience,
that we wear down all obstacles.

We connect to the energies of the fire,
that we can light the way,
that we can act with passion and conviction,
that we burn to reach higher.

Feel the world flow through you;
let it fuel you with strength, patience, truth, and passion.

Final Thoughts

The experience of being involved in this ritual, and many others, has been both fulfilling and enlightening for me. I am proud to have been able to help establish a new tradition based on the principles of the community that now calls Raven's Knoll home. These principles of acceptance, love, equality, and celebration of individuality are what drew me to this community so many years ago. Though sometimes we can lose sight of these qualities from day to day, they are always there. Rituals can help remind us of why we pull together, and why differences are to be treasured, not feared. Being part of a community reminds us that everyone has something to contribute, and everyone needs support from time to time. It reminds us that we are stronger when we help each other, and weaker when we are divided by strife.

I hope to see the Trials of Artemis continue to grow as a proud tradition that will celebrate the strength of women and foster admirable ideals. Many of the women who have so far borne the title of Huntress are inspiring people, protecting those who need it and providing strength and care for the community, and that is what this is really all about.

- - - - - - - - - - ~ - - - - - - - - - -

The following is a list of the women who have
served their community as the Huntress.

2011 - Sarah Ann
2012 - Émilie Boisvert
2013 - Rae Lewis
2014 - Winnifred Owlheart
2015 - Jade Pichette
2016 - Alli Keeley

- - - - - - - - - - ~ - - - - - - - - - -

Kimberly Ross is a freelance copy-editor, a biological anthropologist, a linguist, a humanist, a seeker of knowledge, and a master of all things flammable. She has been a member of the Pagan community for over 20 years, and was a long time staff member for Kaleidoscope Gathering, first as the Fire-keeper for 10 years and then as a Flying Monkey. Her interests are many and varied, and include learning, teaching, making things out of wood (not always for burning), archaeological digs, debating philosophy, and basking in the sun. Her long-term goals include helping people to better understand each other through explorations of language, ritual, and culture, and retiring somewhere warm where she can have great big fires whenever she wants.

A RITUAL OF PROPHECY

by Witchdoctor Utu

The Dragon Ritual Drummers, Niagara Voodoo Shrine, and friends combined to facilitate the main ritual of the 2012 Kaleidoscope Gathering. With the idea of the impending Winter Solstice of 2012 four months away, a date that had existed in the new age and neo-occult world for decades as one that could herald an "end of the world scenario," it seemed a good event to address "through the looking glass," so to speak.

For many of us in the tribe that put the ritual on, it was fairly understood that the infamous date of December 2012 being the end of the Mayan Calendar was not only something that did not warrant panic, but it may have also already happened. While it is true that the Mayan Calendar ended at a Winter Solstice somewhere near 2012, agreed upon by many scholars of such things, the actual date for many years was believed to be vague at best, meaning it could have been a few years before or after December 2012. I firmly believe, and have written about, that it was most likely the Winter Solstice of 2010, which hosted a once in a 500-or-so-year event of a full lunar eclipse in unison. To us, if a lunar calendar that was fairly meticulous in its calculations, and marked lunar eclipses that were visible to the Mayans of the Yucatan, were to end at a point somewhere 500 years into the future, an eclipse that was mathematically known to the priest astrologers of the time was at least very plausible to be such a point.

While to many who study such things, the end of the calendar was most likely just a pragmatic situation of leaving it to be renewed, predicted, and restarted by future priest astrologers who knew that the stars and cycles do eventually shift ever so slightly in the cosmos, and so therefore a new calendar would need to begin; no end of the world, no earth shattering destruction, just a good time to start another cycle.

That being said, many on our planet did not have so much faith in that theory, and so there was a current on Earth that had a tangible sense of panic, ending, and unknown events to begin; with that in mind, we set out to gather our community's positive intentions to be released on the Winter Solstice of 2012.

The main ritual could not have been any closer to "Mexico hot" if we had asked for it; a heat wave in August. As was usual for the KG main ritual, hundreds were in attendance. The intent was explained. We would gather the positive intentions of peace, calm, and the desire to continue and release it at the Winter Solstice a few months away. With the Dragon Ritual Drummers, Eric Mandala, and a host of others providing ambient sounds of drums, gongs, and didgeridoos, and with immense amounts of incense wafting through the air, I walked the circle and described what we endeavoured to do that day. With such a heavy attendance of Southern Ontarians together for the gathering, we also had the South's current reigning Sun King (something similar to KG's Stag King) to provide the Kingly duty of offering sacrifice to the glorious Sun God whose heat was so prevalent. A rather large and ripe watermelon was the chosen offering for the Sun God, along with mead and beer. We prayed to the Sun God, praised his powers, and offered his sacrifice to him; the Sun King (Micheal Roy, a.k.a. Fyre) with sword in full swing sliced the watermelon and held it to the heavens, beer and mead offered in unison. We then passed around the chosen circular mirror that was to be used for this working. It was held to the heavens to capture the Sun God's power and essence; a pact was made. The mirror was also passed around again, while music and fragrance permeated the air, to every single person in attendance at the ritual. Each person looked into the mirror and put in their intentions of peace and calm into it. Why? Because we had planned as was explained to the crowd: to unfurl the mirror at dawn of Winter Solstice 2012, to be held to the heavens once again, but this time releasing the intent of so many, to remind the Sun God of our pact, and that pact was:

We knew the world would not end that morning, but countless globally did not believe as we did. We knew the wheel would continue, but many were not so sure. We released into the world a sense of calm, competence, and responsibility. The world would continue, there would be no need for panic; the Sun God in his guise of judge, jury, and executioner would accept our prayers, and others would not be able to manifest panic and chaos. The witches, warlocks, and Pagans who were in attendance in the hundreds had decreed it so.

We asked everyone in attendance to look to the world of Facebook for confirmation of the workings. Finally, many months from August, in the pre-dawn of the Winter Solstice 2012, members of the Dragon Ritual

Drummers, myself, Fyre, and friends climbed to the highest point on the Niagara Escarpment in our region, awaited the suns rising, and in the cold bitter morning released the mirror's power of heat, warmth, and intent. It was held up to reflect the sun, the pact reiterated; and, like it was custom ordered, no panic, no chaos, no end of the world. As it should have been, as it was decreed.

Were we the only ones that did such workings? Most likely not, but we as a collective–and I say this as one who travels among Pagan and occult communities across the continent for most of the year–were, for sure, the only ones who did such a working on such a scale. Hundreds honouring the Sun God at his most powerful time of the year, when he is closest to us, asking for peace, for continuance, and then releasing that power again at a time while he is much father from us in proximity, no less powerful in his mystery, at Winter Solstice. We posted the photo that morning on the Kaleidoscope Gathering Facebook group page as well as the Dragon Ritual Drummers page, and there was much rejoicing. The sheer numbers of the people involved at Canada's largest Pagan festival, the two-part nature of the ritual spread out over several months, the connection to one of the most unique dates in our current human history, and the intention of community for the wheel to continue to turn, are the reasons why this working deserves to be kept, remembered, and chronicled.

Witchdoctor Utu is the founder of the band the Dragon Ritual Drummers and of the Niagara Voodoo Shrine. He serves the New Orleans Voodoo Spiritual Temple.

HORNED LORD RAP

by Austin Lawrence (a.k.a. MC Auz)

As a person who books bands for Pagan festivals and helps to facilitate Bardic Competitions and fireside sing-alongs, there is a phrase I often hear: "There is not enough Pagan rap." And then, I tell my friends that and they shout: "You liiieeee!" Well, at least some of them do. There are a select few, though, that share my enthusiasm for filling this gaping chasm, currently swirling with a chthonic abyss of harps, Indian flutes, Celtic melodies, African drumming, tonal chanting, and didgeridoo.

As fate would have it, a few years ago I found myself discussing the finer points of how "Old Skool" hip-hop rap battles using end-rhyming shared similarities with Old Norse flyting poetry competitions using alliterative verse, due to their embeddedness in a culture of warrior masculinities, use of modular phrasing, and focus on improvisation. As this was at a men's retreat, this soon turned into a brainstorming session regarding different fantasy Pagan-themed hip hop crews. Witchdoctor Utu and I, in particular, thought up some great ideas. However, the next day, after the short-term memory loss had found its full impact, only one rhyme remained: "As above, yo, so below. As above, yo, so below." (Imagine, of course, that this is accompanied by the hand signs of a "V" of index and middle fingers held aloft with a similar "V" on the other hand pointing to the ground, while feet rhythmically stomp on the ground.)

Years later, friends were putting on the first Witches' Sabbat gathering at Raven's Knoll, where the theme was "The Horned Lord." I had been meditating on the theme for quite a while. One morning, the following rap jumped into my head fully-formed. I furiously wrote it down and performed it at the Bardic Circle at the Sabbat that year. Reprises of the rap were requested at many different Knoll events, over a span of several years. Obviously, some people must indeed have thought: "There is not enough

Pagan rap."

As rap is an oral art form, please read the following aloud; feel free to enlist whoever is in the room with you to improvise by beat boxing. If there are others around, have them help you out with the chorus and hand signs.

I gotta little rap, so here I go …
As above, yo, so below. As above, yo, so below.

Witches call, drink the brew. Moon 'n' magick, Gods to you.
As above, yo, so below. As above, yo, so below.

Goat 'n' pot, brew 'n' wine. Dagger 'n' herb, so divine.
As above, yo, so below. As above, yo, so below.

Dark o' night, in tha forest. Come on folks, chant tha chorus.
As above, yo, so below. As above, yo, so below.

Drum 'n' fire, rise tha song. Us tha witches, we ain't gone.
As above, yo, so below. As above, yo, so below.

[*double time*]

Wind tha circle, feet be stompin'. Drum be thumpin', horns be pumpin'.
As above, yo, so below. As above, yo, so below.

Dancin,' singin,' blesséd be. Naked bodies by tha tree.
As above, yo, so below. As above, yo, so below.

Call tha wild, ta be here. Olden words, jumpin' deer.
As above, yo, so below. As above, yo, so below.

Field found, doe ta stag. Spark o' tines, racks ta brag.
As above, yo, so below. As above, yo, so below.

Nostrils flarin', hooves be switchin'. Beast on beast, humpin', twitchin'.
As above, yo, so below. As above, yo, so below.

Trance induced, show me how. Hornéd Lord, mount me now.
As above, yo, so below. As above, yo, so below.

Goddess movin', three times three. Am I you, are you me?
As above, yo, so below. As above, yo, so below.

Pass tha horn, drinkin' mead. Cake be ate, do take heed.
As above, yo, so below. As above, yo, so below.

[*quietly*]

Learn tha words, to bring tha Spirit.
Spread tha word, so folks can hear it.
As above, yo, so below. As above, yo, so below.

[*shouted*]

Learn tha words, to bring the Spirit.
Spread tha word, so folks can hear it.
As above, yo, so below. As above, yo, so below.

[*spoken*]

Folk be met ... peace out ... Baphomet.

Austin Lawrence is known in the Pagan community as "Auz." He is one of the Stewards of Raven's Knoll and a co-organizer of the Kaleidoscope Gathering. Auz has a Master's degree in Anthropology and is a Heathen who is an oathed Goði that serves as the Keeper of the Raven's Knoll Vé. Auz is also a former Stag King of the Kaleidoscope Gathering. He lives in Ottawa with his wife Maryanne Pearce, his two adult children Kadri Rainne and Joven Wolf, and a menagerie of family pets.

THE FLYTING OF ODIN AND THOR

by Austin Lawrence and Gypsy Birch

Background

Our Heathen forbearers, the pre-Christian Norse and Germanic tribes, transmitted the myths and stories of our religious tradition orally. This was done using rich narratives, as well as a complex and involved poetic culture. To many modern Heathens, who strive to reconstruct the spiritual understandings of the ancients, the reconstitution of the oral performance of religious culture is an important part of the religious revival. It is also the view of a number of modern scholars, foremost among them Dr. Terry Gunnel (1995), that the dialogic poems of the Heathen Norse must be understood to have been presented in a dramatic fashion, and not merely chanted or declaimed.

Although the telling of myths by a single story-teller or the reading of translations of ancient poetry is now fairly commonplace amongst Ásatrúar in this part of Canada, it is rare to see dramatic productions of the lore. To improve on the experiential authenticity of our Heathen spiritual events, Gypsy Birch and Austin "Auz" Lawrence decided to interpret and perform a dialogic piece of the lore as their offering at the Hail and Horn Gathering Skaldry Competition in 2013. They selected the Hárbarðsljóð (The Lay of Grey-Beard) as the poem they would present. It is one of the poems of the Poetic Edda, found in the Codex Regius. The original is an Old Icelandic didactic, flyting poem with figures from Norse mythology. Flyting poems are particularly fun, as they involve the ritual exchange of witticisms and insults. Didactic poems teach and are useful for transmitting lore. In this case Gypsy played the part of the God Óðinn (Odin) and Auz the God Þórr (Thor), mainly because Auz was a big guy with a beard and Gypsy had an eye-patch and a great cloak.

Below is presented, in the left hand column, a translation by Bellows (1936) from the original Old Norse text, and in the right hand column is the modern interpretation. It was decided, in order to make the play accessible to the widest audience (and easiest to undertake in the time that remained before the gathering), to present the interpretation in prose. In addition, some of the original poem was not included in this modern interpretation in the interests of making the play a good length for presentation at the Skaldry Competition.

As Raven's Knoll does not yet have a proper mead-hall in which to hold Heathen rituals and ceremonies, at the Hail and Horn Gathering attendees make due with a number of large tents set up in a line over a massive line of tables and benches. Just off to the side of the tent "hall" is the Keyhole Firepit where the food for the ritual feast (húsel) is cooked and where people gather at night. The Keyhole Firepit is of a functional outdoor cooking-fire type, known from before the Middle Ages. It consists of a circular set of firestones with a rectangular extension of about three times the diameter of the circle on the side. This form echoes the function of the long central hearth-fire that existed in Scandinavian and Germanic longhouses, in a slightly more modern, camping environment.

Auz and Gypsy found it remarkable how little any of the original intention of the text needed to be adapted, and how the hilarious and ribald meaning of the repartee withstood the years. Surrounded by folk seated with horns of drink in hand, bathed by firelight, facing each other across the long hearth-fire, Auz and Gypsy felt the spirit of skalds of old as they brought the joy of the Gods to the folk. From the raucous reaction of the audience, they felt so too.

The Play

Stage directions are identified in italics. Dashes indicate dropped stanzas that were not interpreted.

Bellows (1936) Translation

Thor was on his way back from a journey in the East, and came to a sound; on the other side of the sound was a ferryman with a boat.

Auz and Gypsy Interpretation

Odin stands silent in a black cloak which covers half his face holding a spear. Bearded Thor appears holding a hammer, with a backpack, wearing a belted tunic, but no pants.

Odin is to one side of the hearth-fire, while

Thor is to the other. The audience imagines the hearth-fire to be the river.

Thor called out:

1. "Who is the fellow yonder, | on the farther shore of the sound?"

Thor:

Who is yonder Ferryman across the water? Ferryman! You over there!

The ferryman spake:

2. "What kind of a peasant is yon, | that calls o'er the bay?"

Ferryman:

Who's that peasant over there, calling out to me?

Thor spake:

3. "Ferry me over the sound; | I will feed thee therefor in the morning;
A basket I have on my back, | and food therein, none better;
At leisure I ate, | ere the house I left,
Of herrings and porridge, | so plenty I had."

Thor:

Ferry me across this river! I have lots of food in my backpack to pay you with. I have had many successful hunts in the wood this morning.

The ferryman spake:

4. "Of thy morning feats art thou proud, | but the future thou knowest not wholly;
Doleful thine home-coming is: | thy mother, me thinks, is dead."

Ferryman:

Well, aren't you awfully pleased with your morning wood? Be careful, you have no idea what this evening may hold. Oh, and … your mother's dead.

Thor spake:

5. "Now hast thou said | what to each must seem
The mightiest grief, | that my mother is dead."

Thor:

What? My mother is dead?!

The ferryman spake:

6. "Three good dwellings, | methinks, thou hast not;

Ferryman:

Yup. She's in the ground.* [*Winks.*]
Now look here, how can I expect

132

Barefoot thou standest, | and
wearest a beggar's dress;
Not even hose dost thou have."

you to pay me? I bet you don't even
have a farm. Look at you, you don't
even have pants, how do you expect
me to take you seriously?

** Thor's mother is Jörð, a supernatural
being who is the personification of the
Earth.*

Thor spake:
7. "Steer thou hither the boat; | the
landing here shall I show thee;
But whose the craft | that thou
keepest on the shore?"

Thor:
If it's too difficult for you, I can
show you where to land the boat.
[*Points to a spot on the bank.*] Wait …
Do you even own that boat? Or, are
you just some asshole standing
beside a boat?! But if it's not yours,
whose is it?

The ferryman spake:
8. "Hildolf is he | who bade me
have it,
A hero wise; | his home is at
Rathsey's sound.
He bade me no robbers to steer, |
nor stealers of steeds,
But worthy men, | and those whom
well do I know.
Say now thy name, | if over the
sound thou wilt fare."

Ferryman:
A hero gave me this boat and told
me only to take worthy men into it.
Are you a worthy man? What's your
name?

Thor spake:
9. "My name indeed shall I tell, |
though in danger I am,
And all my race; | I am Othin's
son,
Meili's brother, | and Magni's
father,

Thor:
I am Odin's son, Magni's father. I
am Thor, mightiest of the Gods!
Now, tell me your name!

The strong one of the gods; | with
Thor now speech canst thou get.
And now would I know | what
name thou hast."

The ferryman spake:	*Ferryman:*
10. "Harbarth am I,	and seldom I hide my name."	Grey-beard, I am, and seldom do I hide my name.** [*Winks.*]
	** *In many legends and myths Óðinn goes about in the land of men, Miðgarð, using pseudonyms.*
Thor spake:	*Thor:*
11. "Why shouldst thou hide thy name,	if quarrel thou hast not?"	Why would you hide your name? Unless you actually are just some asshole standing beside a boat.
Harbarth spake:	*Grey-beard:*
12. "And though I had a quarrel,	from such as thou art Yet none the less	my life would I guard, Unless I be doomed to die."	Woah! If you're looking for a fight, I could easily defend myself against you. Unless, of course, it was my fate to die.
Thor spake:	*Thor:*
13. "Great trouble, methinks,	would it be to come to thee, To wade the waters across,	and wet my middle; Weakling, well shall I pay	thy mocking words, if across the sound I come."	Hey! Don't make me come over there, weakling. I might get wet, but I'll kick your ass!
Harbarth spake:	*Grey-beard:*
14. "Here shall I stand	and await thee here;	Hey, I'm even fiercer than that pansy Hrungir. If you really want to come

Thou hast found since Hrungnir died | no fiercer man."

Thor spake:
15. "Fain art thou to tell | how with Hrungnir I fought,
The haughty giant, | whose head of stone was made;
And yet I felled him, | and stretched him before me.
What, Harbarth, didst thou the while?"

Harbarth spake:
16. "Five full winters | with Fjolvar was I,
And dwelt in the isle | that is Algrön called;
There could we fight, | and fell the slain,
Much could we seek, | and maids could master."

Thor spake:
17. "How won ye success with your women?"

Harbarth spake:
18. "Lively women we had, | if they wise for us were;
Wise were the women we had, | if they kind for us were;
For ropes of sand | they would seek to wind,
And the bottom to dig | from the deepest dale.
Wiser than all | in counsel I was,

over here, it might not be worth getting your ... uh ... "pants" wet.

Thor:
I ... What? ... [*Looks down at his lack of pants.*] ... Hey! I beat Hrungnir, that giant blockhead. What have you done?

Grey-beard:
I spent five full winters with the seven sisters on All-Green Island. We would 'wrestle' all day long and I got plenty of 'exercise'.

Thor:
How does a guy like you get seven sisters?

Grey-beard:
Those women liked wise men, and I'm a wise man. That means the women were wise, and the greater knowledge we had of each other, the wiser we got. Trust me, boy; my sword has never been sharper. What have you done that is better?

And there I slept | by the sisters
seven,
And joy full great | did I get from
each.
What, Thor, didst thou the while?"

Thor spake:
19. "Thjazi I felled, | the giant
fierce,
And I hurled the eyes | of Alvaldi's
son
To the heavens hot above;
Of my deeds the mightiest | marks
are these,
That all men since can see.
What, Harbarth, didst thou the
while?"

Harbarth spake:
20. "Much love-craft I wrought |
with them who ride by night,
When I stole them by stealth from
their husbands;
A giant hard | was Hlebarth,
methinks:
His wand he gave me as gift,
And I stole his wits away."

Thor:
I threw a dude's eyeballs into the sky
[*Points to the heavens*], and now
everybody can see them in the stars.
What were you doing when I did
that?

Grey-beard:
I used spells and visited sleeping
witches in their dreams, and
bestowed upon them the gift of my
… fearsome wand.

- - -

Thor spake:
23. "Eastward I fared, | of the
giants I felled
Their ill-working women | who
went to the mountain;
And large were the giants' throng |
if all were alive;

Thor:
Well, I fight giants all the time in
Jotunnheim, protecting Midgard and
all of mankind.

No men would there be | in
Mithgarth more.
What, Harbarth, didst thou the
while?"

Harbarth spake:
24. "In Valland I was, | and wars I
raised,
Princes I angered, | and peace
brought never;
The noble who fall | in the fight
hath Othin,
And Thor hath the race of the
thralls."

Thor spake:
25. "Unequal gifts | of men
wouldst thou give to the gods,
If might too much thou shouldst
have."

Harbarth spake:
26. "Thor has might enough, | but
never a heart;
For cowardly fear | in a glove wast
thou fain to crawl,
And there forgot thou wast Thor;
Afraid there thou wast, | thy fear
was such,
To fart or sneeze | lest Fjalar
should hear."

Thor spake:
27. "Thou womanish Harbarth, | to
hell would I smite thee straight,
Could mine arm reach over the

Grey-beard:
I have caused wars, and all the
nobles who died went to Odin. All
the peasants? They all went [*Gestures
across the river*] to Thor.

Thor:
Be careful with how mighty you are
when it comes to the dead. You do
not want to break the balance
between Gods and men.

Grey-beard:
You spine-less dog. You may be
strong, but you crawled around in a
giant glove afraid to fart or sneeze
lest you wake a sleeping giant.

Thor:
You sodomite ergi-man! I'd beat you
into Helheim, if only I could reach
across this river.

sound."

- - -

Harbarth spake:
48. "Sif has a lover at home, | and
him shouldst thou meet;
More fitting it were | on him to put
forth thy strength."

Grey-beard:
Easy there, big fella. Save that
fighting energy for your wife Sif's
lover.

Thor spake:
49. "Thy tongue still makes thee say
| what seems most ill to me,
Thou witless man! Thou liest, I
ween."

Thor:
You're just being a dick ... and
mean. I don't trust you.

Harbarth spake:
50. "Truth do I speak, | but slow
on thy way thou art;
Far hadst thou gone | if now in the
boat thou hadst fared."

Grey-beard:
Hey, it's the truth. You'd know that
if you were home by now. And you'd
be home by now if you had a boat.

Thor spake:
51. "Thou womanish Harbarth! |
here hast thou held me too long."

Thor:
Look, I've already been waiting here
for too long, and ... —

Harbarth spake:
52. "I thought not ever | that
Asathor would be hindered
By a ferryman thus from faring."

Grey-beard:
I didn't think a God like Thor could
be so easily slowed by a mere
ferryman.

Thor spake:
53. "One counsel I bring thee now:
| row hither thy boat;
No more of scoffing; | set Magni's
father across."

Thor:
Last chance. Row your boat across,
now!

Harbarth spake:

Grey-beard:

54. "From the sound go hence; |
the passage thou hast not."

[Pauses and moves like he is about to do it, but then steps back.] Nope, not gonna do it.

Thor spake:
55. "The way now show me, since
thou takest me not o'er the water."

Thor:
Well, I … *[Sighs.]* … Can you at least give me directions?

Harbarth spake:
56. "To refuse it is little, to fare it is
long;
A while to the stock, and a while to
the stone;
Then the road to thy left, till
Verland thou reachest;
And there shall Fjorgyn her son
Thor find,
And the road of her children she
shows him to Othin's realm."

Grey-beard:
Yeah, you just take the winding road to the fork, take a left, keep going until you come to the foot of the mountain, and then head through the valley. Then, when you find your mommy, she can tell her little bearded baby how to get to Odin's Hall.

- - -

Thor spake:
59. "Short now shall be our speech,
for thou speakest in mockery only;
The passage thou gavest me not I
shall pay thee if ever we meet."

Thor:
[Starts to walk away, but then turns back.] You know what? Even if you did take me across the river, I wouldn't have paid you.

Harbarth spake:
60. "Get hence where every evil
thing shall have thee!"

Grey-beard:
That's fine. I have all I need right here. *[Digs around in his pouch, brings his hand back out and gives Thor 'The Finger'.]*

[Thor exits. Odin removes his hood revealing his face, one eye closed and one eye open.]

Austin Lawrence is known in the Pagan community as "Auz." He is one of the Stewards of Raven's Knoll and a co-organizer of the Kaleidoscope Gathering. Auz has a Master's degree in Anthropology and is a Heathen who is an oathed Goði that serves as the Keeper of the Raven's Knoll Vé. Auz is also a former Stag King of the Kaleidoscope Gathering. He lives in Ottawa with his wife Maryanne Pearce, his two adult children Kadri Rainne and Joven Wolf, and a menagerie of family pets.

Gypsy Birch is a member of Raven's Knoll staff, performing such duties as security and maintenance, as well as assists in organization for multiple events. He is also part of the Flying Monkey security team for the Kaleidoscope Gathering. While he has no defined personal practice pertaining to a particular spiritual path, Gypsy assists followers of many different faiths to ensure that their event or ritual meets the logistical needs of the organizers and attendees.

PRAYERS TO HONOUR
ISIS, SETH, AND ANUBIS

by Anat Thompson

Isis

Lady of Life, Great of Healing;
The beating of your wings caused Osiris to live.
Your name is "Great Throne".
Goddess of Scorpions, Protectress.
Who needs not protection herself.
Whose blood is sacred and great of magic.
You are the first Madonna and child;
Great Mother who nurses her child at her breast.
Goddess of names, spoken in many tongues:

> Eset
> Sel-ket
> Isis of Seubi
> Juno
> Bellona
> Al-Uzza
> Demeter
> Astarte
> Sopdet

You are the most enduring of all the Neteru and your love and devotees are
spread far and wide into the lands of the foreigners.
Honour is given to you Isis, one thousand times over.
We are here today at Kaleidoscope Gathering to honour you and speak
your name. Please grant us your blessings and happiness.

Seth

Great Tribal leader before the North and the South were Unified.
It was your name that Ramses called, for your strength, when he rode into battle.
Vanquisher of Apophis in the Afterworld.
It is your voice we hear in the rolling desert sands.
You are the voice we hear in the roaring thunder,
And it is your staff we see, as a blazing bolt, that pierces the earth.
Mighty Lord of Rain, from a time when the desert to the West was not yet born.
Lord of the Land of Gold, whose flesh is precious.
Lord of the Oasis, whose ancient waters are precious to us.
God of many names, spoken in many tongues:
> Aa-keni
> Ash
> I-gai
> An-ty-wey
> Sutukeh
> Typhoon
> Baal

Honour is given to you Seth, one thousand times over.
We are here today at Kaleidoscope Gathering to honour you and speak your name. Please grant us your blessings and happiness.

Anubis

Psychopomp, who is upon his mountain.
Before the Gods Shrine and in the House of Embalming.
Divine ears that hear our prayers and takes them up to the Divine.
It is you who prepares our bodies.
You who takes our hand on the journey of Going forth by Day,
And leads us to our judgment.
Enduring and Primeval One.
Born of Nephthys.
Anubis, First of the Fist.
Foremost of the Westerners, before Osiris.
Great are your many names:
> Sed
> Wep-iu
> Henty-amen-teu
> Daumutef

Wep-wa-wet
Yn-pu
Hermanubis

Honour is given to you Anubis, one thousand times over.
We are here today at Kaleidoscope Gathering to honour you and speak your name. Please grant us your blessings and happiness.

Anat Thompson is Het Set, Het Eset, Het Ynpu, mother, wife, Pagan, scribe in the service of MAAT, oneiromancer (studier of dreams), dancer, chantress, priestess and servant for the House of Eset and Set.

THE MEMORIAL DREAMCATCHER

by Maryanne Pearce

In 2000, I was part of the Aboriginal children's health team at Health Canada, in Vancouver for a conference. My colleague and I went for a stroll on the Seawall at low tide. There, we found an eagle feather. And another. And another. In all, I gathered 75 eagle feathers as we walked along the tidal zone. These were not the long feathers used in ceremonies, but short, ragged, and about to be swept out to sea, lost forever. But they were still eagle feathers, still sacred. As it was my colleague's moon time, her tradition did not allow her to handle the feathers; they were meant for me. I packed the feathers in cedar, returned to Ottawa and called an Elder. He advised that the feathers were probably lost during a fight between two eagles. He did not know what it signified for me to have found so many, but said the reason would become clear in time.

Seven years later I sent an email to my mother and sisters about my acceptance to the doctorate of laws program and my research on missing and murdered Indigenous women. Instantly, my sister Janette Pearce responded: "I always knew you would figure out what those eagle feathers were for." Janette has always been able to help me see the forest despite the trees. Like the feathers I found, many of the women I write about experienced violence, were a bit tattered, and may have disappeared without a trace, but they are still sacred.

I finished my dissertation in 2013.[i] I had created a database of 3,329 missing and murdered women, of which 824 were Indigenous. Since then, my database has increased to almost 5,000 women, with over 1,100 Indigenous women. The night before I defended my thesis I had a ritual to honour Indigenous women, sex workers, and all victims of violence. Austin, Kadri, Myst, Christina, and Angela joined me for a very intense ritual. This was extremely important to me, but I still felt the need to do something more. The collection of names was important for many reasons not necessary to discuss here, but it was not enough of a memorial. (There are at least three memorials consisting of the list of names from my database. But, as I had created it, I needed to do something different.)

My first thought was to have a cairn somewhere on the property. One polished stone for each name. I was speaking to Courtney Rheaume about this one night and we both started trying to source material. The idea for a cairn was discarded for three reasons. First, if you are ever trying to buy stones in bulk, you will find that this is not easy and people will think you are nuts. The cost was prohibitive. Second, I wondered if a cairn would be too much like a burial mound; I wanted something more hopeful. Third, as I continue to work on the issue of violence against women, the names increase. How would I ever be able to keep it updated?

So, in speaking with Courtney I mentioned a dreamcatcher. She offered to help and came from Montreal one weekend to help. I took the weekend off for this project–something very difficult to do in the weeks before the Kaleidoscope Gathering. I had also mentioned this to Jacqueline (Jax) Thomas and Cat Astrophe, and both had offered to help. None of us had ever done a dreamcatcher before but we had a simple plan and the Interwebs showed us how to do it. The plan was to use sticks from the Knoll as a frame, and put it up somewhere as an organic piece of earth art; about one and a half feet in diameter. Courtney and Jax are artists. Cat is very good with her hands. I tend to tie myself up when using ropes and am not allowed sharp things. An artist I am not.

Then, we started talking around the fire. And the Gods presented inspiration. And so the project got way more complicated and a lot bigger. A lot. Courtney and Austin harvested three birch saplings from a grove on the site. We decided that the dreamcatcher would be placed in a tree, high up behind Staff Camp in a triple-birch tree. We were sure it would fit – who needs to measure organic earth art?

When we laid the three birches onto the ground, the Celtic symbol of the Triple Goddess appeared. We decided to do dreamcatchers within dreamcatchers, with a Triple Goddess dreamcatcher, a centre one, and tiny ones here and there where branches from the birches remained and seemed to want to bend. Jax had beads, I had wool. The four of us each worked a section at a time. It was a lovely, peaceful endeavour. Even though I had hoped to take time off to do this, KG was only weeks away and I had to run off to deal with time-sensitive matters for hours at a time; my friends continued without me.[ii]

We did not finish that weekend. Jax and Courtney finished it during Antici-fest. And, we realized that the intended location for installation would not work–the dreamcatcher was far too large. The Drumming and Dancing Fire Pit was suggested and agreed upon. Installation took place in a flurry. Jax and Courtney were done, and there was time to do it just before KG. Volunteers to carry it were requested over the radio. Before it could be done, I was called out for an emergency. Cat was in registration and couldn't be there and I, much to my regret, didn't think to ask someone to cover her. When I returned to the fire pit, the dreamcatcher had been installed through a great deal of worrisome stretching on ladders, ropes, and inspiration. I conducted an impromptu ritual, repeating the dedication in my thesis:

The memories of all the women and girls
who have died violently.
May justice be yours.

All of the Jane Does.
May your name be restored to you
so you can be returned to your families.

All of the missing women and girls.
May you find your way home safely.

The families and friends of
the murdered and missing women and girls.
May you find peace.

Many of the people witnessing and participating in the installation and ritual had tears in their eyes. This memorial has nothing to do with Paganism, but it is important to me and several of our community. Many people work in prevention of violence against women, have lost friends or family to violence or were otherwise impacted by these issues, or care for humanity. For my three friends who worked with me on this project did so in an act of solidarity with me and my passion. I think of that often. Love and support given through action, for the greater good. That is Raven's Knoll, really. Everyone giving time and talents and thinking of the greater community benefiting from their efforts.[iii]

Endnotes:

i. Pearce, Maryanne. (2013) *An Awkward Silence: Missing and Murdered Vulnerable Women and the Canadian Justice System*. Ottawa University: Faculty of Law. LLD dissertation. See http://www.collectionscanada.gc.ca/obj/thesescanada/vol2/OOU/TC-OOU-26299.pdf.
ii. Pictures of the construction of the dreamcatcher can be found here: http://tinyurl.com/js345yb.
iii. The final dreamcatcher can be viewed at http://tinyurl.com/gu4mur6.

Maryanne Pearce, also known as MA, is one of the Stewards of Raven's Knoll and a co-organizer of the Kaleidoscope Gathering. She holds a doctorate in law, focusing on missing and murdered vulnerable women. Her Master's thesis in Anthropology focused on the Canadian Pagan community. MA is in charge of all the paper involved with RK and KG. She lives in Ottawa with her husband Austin Lawrence, her two adult children Kadri Rainne and Joven Wolf, and various four legged friends.

THE SISTERHOOD OF
THE RED SPIRAL

by Lee A. Farruga

The Red Spiral at Raven's Knoll began as part of a women's retreat created and held by women for women to escape the day-to-day, to re-connect with our spirits, and to gather in sisterhood.

I am honoured to be one of the ladies who helped create this weekend getaway. Its goal was for women to put aside being a mother, student or worker, and to reacquaint themselves with whom they are as a person. We wanted to help women experience themselves as a whole as their Ancestors before and their children after, as part of the larger community, but first and foremost as a brilliant entity of mind and spirit.

The Red Spiral shrine began at the very first retreat. All the women who attended were asked to bring a rock from their homes, or a place that held meaning to them, or simply a stone that was special to them. These rocks were placed from the centre outward with mindful intent to set the spiral as a place of gathering and sisterhood. The connection each woman had with their rock brought that special energy to the space. The rocks were then painted with red ochre–life blood, blood of our ancestors, blood of the land –to seal our intent. The women held hands, sang, chanted, shed a tear or two, laughed, and yelled. We could all feel the incredible force we had set into motion within the Red Spiral.

Each year thereafter, the stone spiral became the focal point to begin and close each weekend retreat. All the new women attending the retreat for the first time were asked to bring a special stone to add to the spiral. And each year another coat of ochre or red paint was added and/or reapplied by the women to their stones to strengthen our original intent. The Red Spiral has grown considerably since that first stone was laid. It is beginning to move into the trees.

It has become a wonderful place to retreat from not only the day-to-day trials and tribulations, but also the turmoil within us that many women have when we wear too many hats. To sit within creates an incredible inner calm. You feel like all the women are there with you, holding you, supporting you, encouraging you. I always leave the Red Spiral[i] with a smile and a different perspective.

It has become a space of gathering and sisterhood–you may enter the Spiral alone, but you are never lonely there, and you will always leave with a calm sense of love and community.

Endnote:

i.   All people that identify as women are welcome at the Red Spiral; it is one's socially-lived gender identity, not their current or former biological sex, that is of importance. It is taboo for men and boys to be at the Red Spiral. Girls, before their womanhood ritual or the age of majority, may be at the Red Spiral in the presence of a woman. Babes-in-arms are welcome with their guardian.

Lee A. Farruga has been a member of the Pagan community for over 25 years. She has explored many Pagan paths over the years as an initiated Wiccan priestess, in ceremonial magic, and in the simple, primal form of nature itself. She has studied the traditions of her Celtic ancestors and she is currently researching her Mediterranean and Sicilian ancestors, their magic, and folklore. She loves her family and community. She also loves to help others and is known as the Geeky Godmother.

THE SORCERER AND THE LIVER

by Blain Hoss

Here is my account of what I experienced at the esoteric rite at the Hail and Horn Gathering in 2014, leading up to and while I sat before the dark, lumbering figure of the Sorcerer who, according to his vestments, demeanor, gesticulations, and speech was enthralled by the otherworldly presence of a being calling himself "Skirnir." After my experience and upon deep reflection, I have no choice but to accept these things for how they were presented to me, for things were said to me by this "creature," things which shook me then and still do to this day. I have no reasons to doubt that this encounter was exactly as it was presented to me: a parlay with Skirnir, the Shining One, vassal to Lord Freyr, most elegant in speech.

Well…maybe not the most elegant, it would seem, but I'll get back to that in a bit.

It was a cool evening in late June. We were all sitting by the Keystone Fire, enjoying the starry night and the various sing-alongs and tales being told. The moon was high, though there were a few wayward clouds. Soon we were told that the time was nigh that we gather in procession, to be led back into the Vé to await some mysterious visitor. In short, it was time for the Esoteric Rite, an annual affair, which follows the earlier raising of the God-pole. It is at this time, roughly 10pm, which some of the gathered folk saunter their way back to the Vé for a chance to peek at the doom and see what the Gods have in store for them. This year was the year of Freyr, as such I was curious as to how this whole "esoteric thing" would play out.

We were led by Linda and her crew from the fire pit in rhythmic fashion, noise makers and all, down the Yellow Brick Road, through the field, through the forest, and eventually up the shrine trail leading to the Vé. The walk was very enjoyable, what with all the stars, fireflies, and microclimatic field-fog. Not much can be said of the procession other than it was very fitting, though one couldn't shake that feeling that at the end of our little jaunt there would be some punctuation. Whether it would be a question mark, exclamation, or some weird hybrid of an interabang remained to be seen.

We made our way into the Vé, most of us having sworn the oath of entrance earlier that day. The God-pole dedicated to Freyr stood in all its glory. That's what I have come to know from earlier years: that just before the Esoteric Rite, the immense presence of the 'new pole in the Vé' is breathtaking. It was hard to focus on anything else in that space beyond the large Godly presence of Lord Freyr.

Once Linda led us into the Vé, we soon joined her and her helpers in the chanting of a piece known as "Gerda's Enclosure." This piece, with all its many vocalic trills and accompanying gestures, is sung so as to erect a secondary 'natural' enclosure within that of the vé-bonds. In a way, to make the area safe for the performance of sorcery, enticing the Sorcerer to come out from his hiding place along with those hidden beings which would assist him in cunning the doom of those there gathered. From my later conversation with the officiate and various helpers, I was informed that the Vé is an "ordered place" set by the Gods as a microcosmic representation of the macro, a venerable axis mundi. Through the chanting and noisemaking of "Gerda's Enclosure," the Sorcerer is enabled with the power to traverse the sacred landscape of the Vé and to interpret the signs within it.

Here is an excerpt of Gerda's Enclosure. I have omitted the gesticulations and key so as to preserve the sacral nature of the chant and the power of the Enchantress:

> You are in seeds,
> You growing all a-round,
> There is no wind,
> Grasp the fine mist on the ground,
> Gone is the sound,
> Ease the way over the land,
> Grow in your way,
> None shall come into my hand,
> For my wall is high,
> And my gate is strong,
> There is none but me,
> Holding the key.

We chanted and chanted, sung and made noise all the while following her lead. Soon, after the chanting had began to quiet, a rustling could be heard from the woods not too far from the entrance of the Vé. It was a tall, say eight-foot figure, shadowy at first, lumbering its way with the help of a smaller attendant clad in some skeletal attire. The primary feature which drew my attention to it, as I peered over my shoulder and continued to chant the piece, was (as I stated) tall. The creature, on what I have confirmed were a pair of home-crafted machinated stilts, wore black pants and a black shirt covered with what I presume to be a plaid shawl. He walked with the aid of his attendant and a large walking stick, each step matching the tempo of the chant, as though we were literally enchanting him out of the woods. What stood out the most though was his 'head covering' or guise. As I was later informed, the Sorcerer felt it important when doing his work to wear an appropriate and specifically crafted disguise so as to provide a high degree of liminality between him and the being he intends to do work with. The guise was dark brown, seemingly camouflage, with a bulbous nose, pointed ears and a long knotted golden beard. His "hair" also of a golden hue was imitative of "elflocks" all matted together at the right side of his head forming a Suebian knot. This was the face of Skirnir.

The first thing I noticed was that there was a hesitation on the part of the Sorcerer as he crossed the threshold of the Vé. Although he was well disguised, I noticed a sudden and rapid change in his countenance, as though at that very moment he ceased being the Sorcerer and "put on" the being of Skirnir. I know this to be fact as once he was added upon his horse-like perch and his dastardly attendant affixed a golden piece of yarn from Freyr's wooden phallus to his elf-lock side knot, one of the first things he said to us was: "Welcome… I have travelled a long long way to be here. You have called me here. I did not come of my own will. To read your doom. I am Skirnir."

The voice was ethereal, unnatural, laboured, old, annoyed, disheveled, haggard, and hoarse, and in no way bright, shining or elegant. If anything he seemed to be rather bemused at what he was witnessing and dumbfounded as to why he was even called to such an event. In short, my general impression of 'this' Skirnir (if that makes any sense at all) was that he really wanted to get whatever we were attempting to do 'on the road' and at his earliest convenience to be on his grumbly way. He addressed us at times in a rudely manner, grunting, snickering, shouting, grumbling and whispering. In general, it was an uneasy meet to say the least.

Then the "show got on the road." As he sat there on his long steed-like bench, he began to stare upon a golden cloth which was laid before him. It was hard to make out in the candle light, but it seemed to be divided into sections by way of linear markings. As I said, these lines were hard to make out and didn't seem to have any rhyme or reason to my knowledge… though I am sure they had purpose to the Sorcerer/Skirnir.

After some time of staring upon the cloth, his attendant came to his side and 'pierced' his shawl or shirt (it was hard to tell) and he let out a shrill which turned to a screech then a low groan…then panting. The whole scene was enrobed in a spasmodic violence, something which the Sorcerer confirmed later on as being penultimate and primordial to his craft. He reached into the slit and with his hand he pulled out a little piece of flesh. This flesh I have been told was a piece of pork liver (or spleen?) which was to be one half of the medium, the other the divided cloth, used to tell us our doom. As a side, I have learned that what he meant by 'doom' was 'judgement, specifically a fate rendered by the Gods', and so Skirnir would tell us what the Gods, specifically Freyr, had decreed for us mortals in their midst.

One by one he called us up to him, or if there were any trepidatious parties, he downright ordered him to come to him. He stated "You called me here, now come learn what you will!" Not all complied, which was their choice of course, but he seemed to grow in ire from then on. When it was my turn, I went up and he instructed me to open my hands. He then plopped the piece of slimy liver into my hands and signaled me to drop it on the garment. What is interesting is that prior to handing it to me, he seemed to mull it about in his own hands, smoothing it and stretching it out. This may have been to 'relax' the organ meat from having held the doom of the person before me, though this is only a guess.

I then plopped it onto the golden cloth and waited. I noticed that at times he would ask people a question, others he did not. Sometimes he whispered something to the individual, at times he made the 'answer' loud enough for all to hear. Some who went before me were angered, others soothed and some muted. As for me, I didn't say a word. The meat plopped down, he looked at it, looked at me and then signaled for me to come to his side. What he told me wasn't whispered, but he didn't make it a loud proclamation either. His words were careful, solemn and evocative. I won't share with you here what was told to me, but as with others who sat at his knee that night, the words spoken were sobering and poignant. I would say that it is not possible for these to have been the words of the Sorcerer himself. For one, no human has the right to say these things. It would be irresponsible as what had been shared with me had life altering consequences, words that I would never have allowed another person to have said to me without repercussion. And so, I have only to accept that what I experienced, what was said to be my doom, were the words of a being called Skirnir and that he did travel a long way to appease our desire for knowledge beyond the ken of mortal humans.

Once most had went up to see him and handled the liver, a still calm came over us all, as though the air pressure had dropped. The stars twinkled a little bit brighter and the winds grew still. Then the being made his wariness known to us all and stated quite exasperatingly that "I am done!"

At that moment the attendant and the Enchantress instructed us to get up and leave. It was a hurried scuttle as he started to groan and make us well aware that he was well past the point of exhaustion and in fact, I would say, sick of our presence. As we left, we all heard a loud cry emanating from the Vé, this signaled Skirnir's departure.

The attendant led us back to the Keystone Fire where we contemplated our dooms. What it all meant. Did it even make sense? About two or three hours after the entire event the Sorcerer regained his mundane vestments and sat in our midst. Accordingly tired and still 'otherworldly' in his gaze. He did not speak much to any of us and could offer little to no clarity on what had earlier transpired as, according to him and his attendants, the entire act was not his own. As he did state to me "I simply set the conditions and made our gathering inviting to the Elf, what transpired thereafter was his own doing."

To conclude, I don't know what more to add. The whole experience was a head-trip. It still doesn't make much sense to me and after some six or seven months since the event, I have not bothered much to question it. It's something which happened. That's all I can say and I was but a mere shadow on the cavern's wall, an actor of sorts…we all were. This would have been my third Hail and Horn Gathering 'Esoteric Rite', one of three otherworldly spectacles to which I was but a fallible pawn in some micro-macro exchange between what is seen and unseen, felt and fraught. All in all, nothing is what it seems and this, like other years, will forever remain a mystery.

Blain Hoss is an avid traveler who has come to Raven's Knoll on a number of occasions. He has found this little piece of Pagan paradise a nice break from the everyday grind. Never one to be pigeonholed or shoehorned into one tradition or another, he has opened himself up to various religious and spiritual experiences such as when he encountered the "Sorcerer and the Liver". It is his hope to never lose the gift of mystery, to find enchantment and magic wherever a chance meet between man and divinity is thought possible.

THE VÉ OF THE JÖTUNNS

by Shane Hultquist

Odin! dost thou remember when we in early days blended our blood together?
When to taste beer thou didst constantly refuse, unless to both 'twas offered?

- Lokasenna (9)

In the early part of 2014 a pole was raised to honour the trickster Loki. After years of debate during the redemoot of Hail and Horn Gathering, it was established that Loki would never be voted to hold a place in the main Vé. A shrine trail was planned leading from the main drumming fire pit to the main Vé and one of the first stops on this trail is where the Loki pole was raised.

Many of the friends of Loki discussed the need to honour Him as Odin is honoured in the main Vé. Based on the evidence of the Poetic Edda (quoted above), Odin and Loki are blood brothers and when a drink is offered to Odin, one should also be offered to Loki as well. It was decided that a vé would be erected around Loki's God-Pole as well.

Shane was put in charge of organizing the ritual that would see the new Vé erected in that space and with the assistance of many, the Vé poles were found and prepped.

Upon arrival at the location of the future site of the Vé, it was determined that the holes would be quite difficult to dig for these posts. In a compromise, the poles were shortened so the holes would only need to be dug roughly two feet deep. Using a spade shovel, the holes started to appear one at a time around the Loki pole and mound. However, on the fifth hole, the shovel promptly snapped at the base. It was now as useless as a wet noodle for our purposes. This would come to be the first test of the sly one in preparing his home. After countless discussions and many hours, we

155

decided that there was no way to dig the remaining four holes (to make a total of nine) so we would instead use the trees that formed a bit of a natural vé around the mound.

The call was made for the ritual to begin and people began making their way to the area. The turnout was much larger than anticipated.

Once the folk had gathered on the shrine trail in front of the Vé , Shane stepped forward to the pole and spoke some words in Loki's ear, poured a libation to him and then turned to the crowd:

> The Vé we are about to erect will surround the pole that was carved in the image of Loki. This vé will serve as his home, his sacred space and his place of worship. This is the home of the Jotunns, the Utgard, the outsiders.
>
> Each post we raise will be dedicated to one of the nine worlds.

He explained how they would proceed with each individual post, threading the rope through the rings and dedicating each post to a different aspect of the Jötunns. At each post, a libation was poured to the ground and others were welcome to participate in this as well and several took him up on that offer.

> To Helheim, realm of the dead. Loki's daughter rules this realm and maintains control of those that have died dishonourably.
>
> To Svartalfheim, realm of the dark elves. Home of the dwarves who crafted all the treasures of the Gods for Loki.
>
> To Muspellheim, realm of fire and heat. Home of Surt, wielder of the great flaming sword, shining brighter than Sunna herself.
>
> To Vanaheim, realm of the Vanir. Home of Njord who was wed to the Giantess Skadi as weregild for the death of her father Thjazi.
>
> To Niflheim, realm of ice and cold. Birthplace of Ymir, the first of the Giants.
>
> To Alfheim, realm of the light elves and nature Gods. Home of Laufey, mother of Loki.
>
> To Asgard, realm of the Aesir, home of the Gods. The wall

surrounding Asgard was built due to the cunning of Loki and also beget Odin's steed Sleipnir.

To Midgard, realm of man and playground of Loki. It is here the Loki enjoys causing strife amongst kith and kin for his own amusement.

To Jötunnheim, realm of the giants. Homeland to those who will be worshipped in this place.

Once all the rope had been threaded and the Vé erected, an invocation to Loki was performed:

> Loki, Beloved of Sigyn,
> Brother of Odin, Mother of Sleipnir, Father, Husband, Friend,
> Come to us today as teacher, Gift-giver, our Honored Guest,
> Come, and tell us the truths we need.
> Shapeshifter, teach us how to change ourselves, to be more than we think we should be.
> Let us peer behind our masks, and know our true selves, and accept them,
> As we accept You at our table.
> In the spirit of Gebo,
> we offer You a gift for Your gifts, of cakes and mead.

Then each individual (if they chose) were welcomed to offer a libation to Loki in whatever form they desired.

Once the libations were complete, we moved to an open area where the eyes of Loki could look upon us. A small fire was burned in a fire bowl for the guest of honour. At this point a small play depicting the story of Loki cutting Sif's hair and getting the gifts of the Gods from the dwarves was performed. Austin played the role of the dwarves; Brynn played the role of Sif; Paul was Thor; Linda, Doug, and Shane all played the role of Loki, in turn.

A fun time was had by all during the interactive performance when audience members were included in the story. After the end of the story, we thanked Loki for his presence there and the ritual ended. The Vé would be visited many more times over the next week as Kaleidoscope Gathering took hold of the land.

In the coming years, more poles will be raised in the space to honour those that would not be honoured in the main Vé including Hel, Jötunns and others. It is a safe space to give your offerings without judgement.

Shane Hultquist lives in Ottawa and is a self-professed Geek. He has spent many hours building the virtual web of wyrd for the Knoll and the events that happen there. He has also spent many years on staff at the Kaleidoscope Gathering. These days he spends most of his time on various grass surfaces promoting the sport of Kubb for www.kubbcanada.com.

TO DANCE WITH FIRE IN WONDERLAND: BRINGING LOKI TO THE KNOLL

by Jacqueline Thomas

Austin and I had just left Douglas, ON, when he mentioned possibly wanting to carve a God Pole for Loki. Inwardly I balked at the idea. However, knowing our community, it made sense to have Loki grace the Knoll. I knew I was going to be at the Knoll the next weekend helping with the Dreamcatcher, so I offered help if he wanted. Honestly, what I really wanted to see was the actual carving process of a God Pole. Little did I know that I was about to dance with fire down the rabbit hole and come out the other side with no idea what just happened, although whatever was to happen, it would be life altering.

Starting that night, the dream began, and with each passing night it grew in intensity. This type of dream is not new to me. This one though was so very different; to say the dream unnerved and baffled me would be a complete understatement.

The dream was always the same. I am sitting in a clearing next to a crouched figure who is muttering incomprehensibly as they scrape at a stone. I try to lean forward and sneak a peek at what they are doing; that is when I start to notice the thick warm liquid running down my face. At first it was just a trickle, although by the end I felt like someone was pouring warm water down my face. I try to lift a hand to rub my eyes, but my hands won't move. The thick liquid stung my eyes and gave everything a reddish haze. I start to feel like I could not get a breath in and began to gasp and splutter. That was when the figure noticed my presence. They turned to look at me, slowly leaning into my face to study it muttering, never stopping. Suddenly, there was a hand on my face, tracing shapes in the blood running down the same way a small child would play with finger

159

paints. With a final swipe of their hand they cleaned the blood off my face and smacked it down upon the stone.

After their hand smacked on the stone, I would wake and end up staring at the ceiling for the rest of the night. The dream continued for seven nights, never making sense and growing stronger, almost urgent, with each passing night. By the Saturday of the next weekend I was truly ready for it to either make sense or stop. The lack of sleep was playing havoc on my personality. Little did I know that things were about to change and get very interesting. Very interesting indeed.

Saturday morning started lazily, the smell of wood smoke already drifting in the air as the Firemongers prepared for their day ahead. Those of us working on the Dreamcatcher gathered at the Rookery after breakfast and began discussing how we were going to achieve weaving the giant piece and going about trying to decide a good location to hang it once finished. Just after lunch, Austin (who had been preparing the God Pole over by the Standing Stone) came over and showed me a printout of the Snaptun Stone which is believed to be an image depicting Loki. I said I thought it was a good choice and agreed with the alterations that he wanted to do, but at this point 'who will carve it' was still not my interest. After a brief chat we both returned to our jobs. Looking back though, if I had known that the world would turn on its side fifteen minutes after that conversation, I would have grabbed a snack and gone pee.

It started with a tug, a gentle feeling that I wanted to go to the God Pole. I ignored it and continued to focus on my task, but it didn't go away. This was not simple curiosity. Soon the gentle tug became an urgent pulling and the *want* to go became a 'You have *no choice*, GO!" I had enough time to let the ladies know I was just headed over to see what Austin was up to and I would be back shortly. My walk turned to a gazelle-like sprint, my heart pounded with excitement, and it was at this point when I knew someone else was *with* me, I was not alone anymore. I remember walking up to Austin who, by this point, had sketched the face and begun the carving. There was about a minute of small talk, and then the catalyst happened: Austin asked if I wanted to give it a go with a bit of the carving and I said "Yes".

After learning a few basics of carving and hearing the dirty jokes about me straddling the pole, I began the slow meticulous process of making sure everything was just so for the one who would inhabit it. Even though I knew *someone* was there with me, there was never a voice or a divine intervention moment. Instead, I got strong emotional responses to whether they liked something or not. They did not want a curly mustache as planned; it upset them. They did not want the carving lines too thick; when my chisel slipped, taking a larger chunk than planned, I knew they were angry. They were very happy that the stitches in the lips matched the grains and cracks already existing in the wood, and they made sure I knew they did not want a beard. It was dinnertime before I remember looking down at the finished piece; I just hoped I could convince Austin that this is how the pole needed to look. Thankfully, he agreed with everything I had done and said it was time to store the pole until a time when it could be raised.

This is about when I noticed that my feelings had changed and maybe, just maybe, I had been wrong to disbelieve in Loki. Suddenly I knew I had to fight to get this pole raised that day, for whoever was with me needed it that way. It was in that moment I knew we had opened the proverbial box and we needed to see this to the end. The pole had to be raised. It was part of the dance. Within a moment of my voicing that we needed to keep going it was like an infection spread through our small trio. Gypsy was first to join in that we needed to raise the pole, but Austin was not far behind. It looked like Loki would be raised at nightfall and there was a lot to do to prepare.

Austin had originally wanted to paint the face with ochre, but when he returned from his search there was no ochre to be found. So while Gypsy was in charge of firing (charring) the end of the pole, Austin and I went to see what we could find. We found Louisiana hot sauce, ash and coal from the Keyhole firepit, and aquavit, which we mixed together into a black paste. I used the mixture to carefully paint the face using a thin twig as my brush.

As the time drew closer and closer, I felt the same excitement growing again. I knew whoever was there was growing impatient. They wanted to get things going, no more waiting. When we arrived at the site, we all just looked about at each other, but it was time to start. The impatience was growing to a crescendo level. I filled my lungs and called out "Come and HAIL LOKI!" which was echoed by a small voice from behind "or not…".

Again, the impatient and desperate feeling swelled inside of me, like a starved animal desperate to get the food just in front of it. As we began, we started by placing some offerings into the hole made for Loki. I could feel my heart quicken and my breathing deepen. It was time. The pole was lowered into place and slowly erected into position. People cheered and hailed. I was so caught up that I didn't notice that the intense feelings and presence of *someone* had gone. We continued by telling the Jötun to "fuck off", that we now had "Loki to protect us" from them, and then we got Loki drunk on offerings. I now understand why Loki did not want a carved beard, because after just a few months of use there have been so many offerings on the pole that the wood has now stained in the shape of a beard. When all was said and done, our large group headed to the bonfire at the main fire pit to celebrate and relax.

I felt so relieved that everything had gone so well, but there was a noticeable emptiness within me. Something of me and "the who" were gone. It was at that time when Austin came and quietly gathered Gypsy and

I from the fire. We snuck off away from the large group and he told us about how he had gone back to see the Loki pole and had heard coyotes madly yipping like hyenas up near the Vé. It was then that sticks began to snap around us, and we could hear snuffles and yips from the bush just metres ahead of us. We decided at that point that it was time to head back to the safety of the crowded bonfire and to come back in the morning to check things out. For the rest of the night though, all three of us kept a close eye on the berms, almost sure that at some point the coyotes would crest them. First thing the next morning, I headed to the shrine trail. There were coyote footprints all over Loki's mound and the surrounding area. I knew for sure at that point that Loki had made himself at home at the Knoll.

As we packed up to head home, that is when I noticed the physical side-effects of carving Loki. Even though I had placed most of the pressure on my knees while carving the pole, being very careful not to rest my body or skin on the actual wood, from my collar bone to my inner thighs was a continuous dark black-and-purple bruise. It would take a month or so to realize the emotional and mental side effects, though. I was no longer unhappy with life, and I was no longer anxious and stressed about everything. I felt free and light for the first time in my life. My ego, world, and beliefs changed this summer at the Knoll, and I wouldn't change a thing.

Hail Loki ... or not.

Jacqueline Thomas is Single Momma Bear. Lover of food. Minecraft Addict. Heathen. Artist. Girl with a story. Survivor.

RAISING THE STANDING STONE

by Julie Desrosiers

First comes the discovery. Shortly after the thought of raising a stone is spoken, the stone appears. On land that is sandy and swampy, where no other stones larger than a loaf of bread can be found, there it is. Hidden but not. Covered by a single layer of leaves, in the scrap pile. This rock is tall and flat and perfect for raising. There is talk that it was once the door sill to an old house, but how it arrived, and what purpose it served remains a mystery. A new purpose is awaiting it.

The word travels to Thornhaven Grove that a stone has been found. For years, the Grove had been contemplating moving and standing stones to create a henge on their land. The main obstacle had always been finding the people to help move them. Now, the Grove is faced with a joyous confluence of circumstances. For this summer, the Grove is hosting the first ever gathering of Ar n'Draiocht Fein Druids in Canada, at the Three Rivers Festival at Raven's Knoll. To this new festival will come the people to raise the stone.

The stone is prepared for its journey, dug from the earth and placed in a cradle of rope under the trailer pulled by the tractor Duchess. Although most of the work is done by instinct and best guesses, moving the stone into the cradle is easy, and through the power of iron horses, the stone is brought to its new home.

The location where the stone is to be raised is also prepared. A hole is dug, deep and narrow, to accommodate more than half the length of the stone. The earth will be the foundation and the prop that will keep the stone upright for generations upon generations.

The people collect around the hole, and the stone, and begin the slow and steady work of raising it. The folk move together, pushing and pulling, using the powers of leverage and teamwork to get the stone into place.

They use simple tools as their ancestors did, and look out for one another's safety. In less than an hour, the stone is erect, a silent testament to the strength of the earth and the ingenuity of humankind.

Already, the earth around the stone is humming, broken and changed into its new shape. Now the people process to the place, ringing a bell to announce the making of a new sacred site. The standing stone is hallowed with fire and water, to make it a fitting vessel for the portal that is about to be created. Then, the Ancestors are called in. First to be called are the Ancestors of the land at Raven's Knoll, those who lived and took sustenance by the waters of the Bonnechere. Then the folk call upon the Ancestors of Spirit, those who inspire and teach from beyond the veil. Lastly, the folk call upon the Ancestors of Blood, those grandmothers and grandfathers going down through the generations, going back to time without memory, letting their blood be the link to the first people.

"The Ancestors are with us," the words are spoken," they are in us, in the earth we stand on, in the stone before us. In raising this stone as our ancestors did, we remember them more, and they draw closer to us." The words ring out in the circle of the folk, and underneath the words is the sound of power rising from the earth, a slow and steady beat.

A bowl of red ochre mixed with olive oil is brought forward. Red like blood, thick and visceral, the ochre symbolizes both life and death, and the connection that the folk have with the Ancestors, whose blood runs through their veins. Mined from the earth, the ochre is also a link to the land–it is holy dirt. Now it becomes a magic tool, to mark the stone as sacred. One by one, the folk place their hand in the ochre and press their hand onto the stone. It becomes covered in hand prints, all different sizes and shapes. Coated in red, it is transformed into a sacrifice, a permanent shrine to honour the old ones.

As the last person places her hand on the stone, the space pulsates with energy and radiates with the warmth of community. The Spirits of the Ancestors are co-mingled with the Spirits of the folk, and the portal is made. To celebrate, the folk share in the blessing cup, drinking deeply of the gifts bestowed upon them. They sing joyfully:

> Pour the waters, raise the cup.
> Drink your share of wisdom deep.
> Strength and joy now fill us up.
> As the Elder ways we keep.

Now the ritual is almost ended, and so thanks are given to the Gods, the Ancestors and the Spirits of the land, for watching over the folk during the raising and blessing of the stone. As the crowd disperses, individuals come forward with their own offerings, and the air becomes redolent with incense and honey. The Standing Stone, once a focus for community, now becomes a space for private connection, as each person comes forward and whispers their prayers, offers their sacrifices. The portal is not closed, but stands ever-present for the people of Raven's Knoll to speak to their ancestors.

Julie Desrosiers is an initiated priestess of the Odyssean Wiccan tradition and the Senior Druid for Thornhaven Grove, within *Ar nDraoicht Fein* (ADF). She is one of the founders of Three Rivers Festival, the ADF Canada East Regional Gathering, which is held at Raven's Knoll. Julie has served her Pagan community in numerous ways throughout the years, including as an event organizer, volunteer, ritualist, and public speaker. She was head of registration at Kaleidoscope Gathering for five years. She is also licensed by the Province of Ontario as a wedding officiant, and has performed various rites of passage for the greater Ottawa pagan community as part of her own vocational calling. She is most interested in ritual construction, ritual as art (and vice versa), and the synthesis of the mind, body and spirit in ritual work. Julie is also the custodian of Thornhaven, a plot of land (18 acres) that is being actively naturalized and consciously imbued with sacred energy, to serve as a place of powerful worship and communion with the Gods, Ancestors, and the Spirits of the Land.

LISTENING

by Angela Grey

For me, festivals are always a bit of a blur. My memories of them tend to be happy swirls of colour, snatches of conversation and song, a kaleidoscope of faces. So much to see, so many dear friends to hug, and never enough time to do it in.

In some ways, I actually prefer the work weekends. When all the regulars get together to pitch in and help maintain the place we love, the pace is slower, and there's more time to talk. I've met some of my closest friends while gathering sticks along Bogside or weeding the beach, and although we work hard, we always take time out for a joke and a snack. It's not just the people I get to spend more quality time with, though. It's the land itself. I've always relished the role of being a steward. Of tiding up the campsites, tucking away lawn chairs, and sorting the recycling. On those calm, steady weekends, there are more quiet moments to breathe the air, lounge in the sunshine, and appreciate what we have.

One particular Kaleidoscope Gathering, lounging was the furthest thing from my mind. I was on staff that year, working as a Troll. Cleaning bathrooms and collecting garbage may not seem like spiritual activities, but it was what the land and my community needed. And I still got to be a steward of sorts, albeit a very dusty one. I had my ear glued to the radio, dashing from call to call; joking with my teammates as we cheerfully took care of the needs of hundreds of guests. But then there came one of those rare and wonderful moments: a kind of a lull; a pause in the frenetic activity. A quiet place between calls, when there was nowhere I needed to be, and nothing I really needed to do.

I was wandering Diagon Ally, browsing the incredible array of wares. All around me people were chatting with friends, strolling to workshops, and bantering with the vendors. I thought idly that I might wander over to

Helmut's Forge. He'd mentioned that he'd brought some particularly nice knives that year, and I was eager to see them.

I happened upon the table where Auz's mom, Hanne, had set out a variety of unfired clay tiles. Hanne is an incredibly talented potter, and examples of her work can be found peeping out of nooks all over the Knoll. That year, she was raising money by donating dozens of patterned tiles that she had created. For a couple of dollars, you could pick a tile and put a personal message on it. After the festival, the tiles would be fired and used to decorate the walls of the comfort station. I'd been wanting to make one, but had nearly forgotten to do it. It seemed like I would get my chance after all.

I carefully looked over my choices, and chose one with a design I liked. Then I paused, thinking about what I wanted to say. What was the message I wanted to leave for the people who came to visit the land that I loved?

As I pondered, I gazed up over the riot of canopy tops at the stunningly blue sky. I realized that, under the murmur of voices, I could hear the soft hissing of the wind in the pine trees, and see the rich puffs of green gently swaying to and fro. I heard the chittering of a squirrel as he scampered amongst the branches; and I realized that what I wanted was for other people to have those moments, too.

I leaned over my tile and carefully wrote, "The Land is Listening". Just as I finished signing my name underneath, a ruby flash darted before my eyes, and a bright red dragonfly settled on my writing hand.

Now, the Knoll has dragonflies in their thousands, in colours ranging from light turquoise to deep sapphire. But never before, and rarely since, had I seen a red one.

It seemed to stare up at me for a dozen heartbeats, tail barely brushing the pen I still held. I scarcely breathed, and then, as suddenly as it had come, it alit, and flew off into the dappled sunshine. I stared after it for a long time before the crackle of my radio brought me back to earth, and I headed off on another call.

Some years later, I got a red dragonfly tattooed on my calf. Whenever I glance down at it, I smile. It's my personal reminder that the land really is listening. And sometimes, if you're very lucky, it will answer you back.

Angela Grey grew up in a small hamlet in Northern Canada, surrounded by a colorful assortment of homesteaders, hunters and tradesmen. Throughout her teenage years, she spent most of her spare time exploring "the Bush" on horseback, or camping with her family. As an adult, her Wiccan practice is firmly rooted in working with the local landscape. When she's not roaming the forests of Central Canada, she can usually be found curled up with a book in front of the nearest fire.

A COMING OF AGE CEREMONY
... FOR TWO!

by Courtney Rheaume with Alex Thomas

I was sitting around the bonfire in the company of great friends, sharing some drinks, laughter, and good conversation; a typical summer's evening at Raven's Knoll.

It was that night, in front of the roaring fire that an idea was birthed, a decision was made, and a very pivotal moment in two special girls' lives would soon thereafter come to be.

This particular weekend was Fire Monger's weekend, in which I happened to be at Raven's Knoll visiting. I was not partaking in the weekend's event, but was helping on another special project with MA. To my surprise and delight, I ran into my very good friends Alex and Emily at the fire that night.

During our random discussions catching up with one another we, as most parents tend to do, had reverted our conversation to our girls. What new adventures they were having, what new milestones we were facing with the teenage years, puberty, and all that fun stuff that makes our daughters twitch if they are within earshot. Both Alex and I have been single-parenting our daughters all of their lives, so the similarities are usually in abundance. Our daughters are also close friends and of the same age, which is an additional bonus for discussing the harder topics (hormones, boys, "what do you do if", etc.).

Maryanne Pearce had been speaking with Alex about having a Coming of Age Ceremony for Emily to celebrate her reaching puberty, and with me soon to be bringing my daughter Haley to the Kaleidoscope Gathering for her first time this summer, Maryanne suggested to perhaps have the ceremony for both of them together. Alex and I fast agreed to this as we both wanted to hold the ceremonies for our girls, but hadn't given much thought to the where or how, and Emily was thrilled with the idea of having Haley with her. As outgoing as our girls are, they are both shy when it comes to being in the limelight. So having each other for support was a welcomed idea. We needed only to ask my daughter if she was alright with the idea, and it would be a go. The conversation soon changed direction, and the topic was left alone for the evening.

Excited upon my return home to my daughter, I ran our idea over with her during dinner. She was confused at first, not knowing what the ceremony entailed…but then overjoyed to hear that Emily would be with her. Now that she was on board, it was time to put my head together with Alex's and plan our daughters' ceremony!

Now, for those readers who might not be familiar with the term "Coming of Age Ceremony," it is a ceremony or ritual dedicated to transitioning children into early adulthood. Typically, it will be held soon after the child has hit puberty. It is also known by other names such as Blood Ceremony, Moon Party, and Rites of Passage Ceremony. This is celebrated by many cultures worldwide, and the ceremony itself varies as does the age of the child recipient. Sadly, western culture doesn't celebrate this milestone as much as other cultures, but it is fairly widespread within the Pagan community. It signifies the day that we, as parents, present our daughters or sons to the community as a young lady or young man rather than 'our little girl' or 'our little boy.' The separation factor is present and the children are then viewed and recognized as an equal member of the community, as a fellow Sister or Brother respectively, and their actions are now consequential as they are spreading their wings into adulthood.

Plan the ceremony…Oh Gods! How do we go about planning this ceremony?!

For a brief background on our daughters, both are 13 years old. Both, as mentioned earlier, have been raised in single-parent households as only children. And neither, as much as their parents (Alex and I) are Pagan, practice the Craft. They are familiar with and known throughout the Pagan community, and they are familiar with our beliefs and some of our customs, but we never pushed our beliefs on our girls, as we valued them having the rights to their own beliefs. So how do we plan a ceremony for them that will incorporate some of our Pagan ways, but still be comfortable and understandable for them?

Well, in typical fashion of Alex and I, we planned to break down the barriers of the normalities and do things our own way! Oh, that sounded great in theory, only this time we didn't have a clue! We hadn't had the pleasure of these ceremonies ourselves. I personally was handed a box of tampons, told to read the instructions, and given a curt "Congratulations, you are a woman now." Short, barely sweet, and to the point. Both Alex and I had been to these ceremonies for our friends' children, though our experiences were very different from one another.

It was time to do some research, it seemed! So we did what most people do: we called upon our good friend Google!

That experience: fair warning to anyone in the predicament of planning such a ceremony or ritual for the first time, it can be horrifying, hilarious, helpful, or a nightmare. If you want to laugh (as in roll on the floor, cannot breathe, tears falling from your eyes laugh), please watch the YouTube video at www.tinyurl.com/pvfsyqk. Show your daughters this before their ceremony. I assure you that no matter what you do for their Coming of Age Ceremony, they will be forever grateful that it wasn't a Moon Party like that! Alex and I are still laughing over that video, and it helped ease our fears of planning the ritual for our girls.

We had agreed from the beginning that the ceremony had to be geared towards our girls: their tastes, their personalities, and above all we wanted them to realize that menstruation should not be feared, looked upon as gross, dirty, or wrong. That it should be celebrated, and recognized as an important and special transition. To embrace the change, welcome it and feel proud about reaching this milestone of becoming young ladies.

Neither one of us were partial to the traditional 'Only Woman Guest List.' Some of the most pivotal and important role models in our daughters' lives were men. Why shouldn't they be allowed to share in such a special day? We do not disagree with the traditional way of doing things, it just wasn't right for our daughters.

Another common occurrence it seemed in our research was the lean towards basing the ceremony around the menstrual portion, and having red themes throughout. That alone would gross out our girls, as they are both shy to begin with. No need for making them uncomfortable on their big day! We wanted them to take away a sense of communal belonging, self-pride, and perhaps the gift of knowledge from their Elders. We wanted them to know that they were not alone in this milestone, and they are surrounded by loved ones who will be there along the way to help them in their journeys to becoming young woman, be it through advice, guidance, love, or friendship.

After hours of searching, jaw dropping moments, 'what on Earth did I just read?' moments, and some serious giggle-attack moments, we came across a very simple ritual that was performed for a young woman that incorporated her, her mother, and her guests, as well as having all the principles we were looking for. In reading it over, we were able to tweak it to include quarter calling, calling of the God, the Goddess, the Ancestors, creating of Sacred Space, creating a circle, and having offerings that our girls could give back to the Earth as a part of themselves in thanks. It was perfect! All we needed now was a location, a date, and a guest list! Oh, and to rewrite the ceremony to the likes of our girls. Easy enough, right?

Location, location, location! Where can we hold this ceremony that is special and magical? Well, Raven's Knoll of course! But there are so many Sacred Spaces…where on the land would be best suited for such a ceremony? In my discussions with Alex, I asked about the Birch Grove.

Five years ago during the very first Kaleidoscope Gathering held at Raven's Knoll, I was privy to attend the first Women's Ritual on the land. Together we women laid our footsteps for generations to follow within the sacred space of the Birch Grove. We made the space our own, and created the Women's Shrine which still stands today just outside of the Grove. It was a pivotal ritual in my life and, to this day, I hold that space dear to my heart, hearing our voices singing in the gentle breeze of the birch trees' branches every time I visit the space. I had hoped for our daughters to be welcomed into the Pagan community as women within the very same space that we had created. With the approval of Alex and MA, our location was set.

The guest list was the easiest part, and happily accepted with our non-traditional invite to certain men of stature in our daughters' lives.

Now to tweak that ceremony, incorporate our guests to be part of it, and, oh yes…a date.

As busy as Alex and I both tend to be for Anticifest,[i] we felt it better suited for the girls to have it then, as there are far less people on site so the intimacy would be greater. Most of those who we were inviting luckily attend Anticifest and were able to make it.

The planning, however, started long before! From the offerings, to who was doing what during the ceremony, to their gifts, to what they were wearing, to the cakes and ale offered afterwards, every bit of the ceremony was planned from start to finish so we wouldn't stress as much the day-of. Well, that was what we had hoped for anyways!

The ritual-writing itself was a back-and-forth process of consistent editing with Alex and I until we agreed with one another on the final edition.

- - - - - - - - - - ~ - - - - - - - - - -

The Ceremony

Ritualist A…….We have come together today to welcome two new ladies into our circle. Girls, come and join us and bless our gathering with your presence.

Our daughters' mutual friend enters the circle with Emily and Haley, bringing them to the altar at the center of the circle. She had her Coming of Age Ceremony the summer prior. Typically, unless their friends have already had a ceremony of their own, they aren't allowed to attend a ceremony of this sort, so as not to wreck the experience for themselves.

Ritualist B ....We are now creating Sacred Space, to bring the blessings of the Elements, Gods, and Ancestors to this ceremony. Let us all face in the direction of each calling.

Guest...............*With everyone facing North, the direction of Earth, the guest calls to the Spirits of the Knoll in their own manner.*

Guest...............*With everyone facing East, the direction of Air, the guest calls to the Spirits of the Wind in their own manner.*

Guest...............*With everyone facing South, the direction of Fire, the guest calls to the Spirits of the Hearth Fire in their own manner.*

Guest...............*With everyone facing West, the direction of Water, the guest calls to the Spirits of the Bonnechere River in their own manner.*

Maryanne........*As Priestess, Maryanne Pearce, calls the aspects of the Goddess, in her own manner.*

Austin..............*As Priest, Austin Lawrence, calls the aspects of the God, in his own manner.*

Ritualist B ....*The officiate calls to the Ancient Grandmothers of both Blood and Spirit, to invite their blessing to the ceremony.*

All of the guests walk around the circle with incense creating the sacred space. Two guests then stand aside just outside of the outskirts of the circle to hold safe the sacred space.

The Vessel and the Gift

Alex ....We want to tell you both a story. It is the story of all of us women here, and today it becomes your story as well.

Before your birth, I and your mother carried you each within us, just as your Grandmas carried us, and their mothers carried them. Before them came a long line of women all the way back to the beginning, when humans were emerging distinct from the rest of life on Earth.

Courtney.........All these past women since time immemorial carried within them the spark that would become you. Your existence is a testimony to their labours. Within each of you, every cell of your body, there exists a genetic link, unbroken, to these women. It is literally the same as that of most ancient women in your line. It is their gift to you.

Alex ....Now you join this long line of women. It's time for you both to take your place. You two have come into full womanhood.

Courtney.........Your body now has the potential to be a vessel to carry the next generation into being. But regardless of any future generations, you are a vessel for your own soul. You are a vessel for your creativity, your thoughts, wishes, hopes and dreams.

Ritualist A.......Emily and Haley, laying before each of you on the altar is a bowl. Please stand and hold the bowl out in front of you.

Ritualist B.......As we each pour an offering into your bowl, we offer you a gift. Please accept these gifts in the spirit of which they were given.

The youths position themselves with the bowls. In turn, Ritualist B calls up each of the pairs of offerings, while Ritualist A hands each pair of guests an offering to give to the girls.

Guests ....This oil symbolizes richness. I wish for you a life rich in love. May you grow in this richness every day of your life.

Guests ....In ancient times, wine was used as medicine. This wine symbolizes health. I wish for you a long and healthy life.

Guests ....This water symbolizes clarity. I wish for you the ability to see situations clearly, and to discern the truth. May you always see your truth clearly.

Guests ....This milk symbolizes nurturing and comfort. May you always find what you need to sustain you. May you find comfort and sustenance when you need it.

Guests ....This honey symbolizes the sweetness of life, joy, and happiness. I wish for you a life filled with happiness and joy.

May you be blessed with life's sweetness.

Guests .... This pinch of salt represents the salt of your tears. With it, we recognize that life is not always easy. Like everyone, you will have times of sadness, difficulty, pain, and grief. May you always have friends to hold you and help you through the tough times, may the joy of your life far outweigh the sadness, but no matter what the future has in store for you, may you always grow in inner strength and courage as you walk through life's journey.

Guests .... This sage represents wisdom. I wish for you a life of ever-growing wisdom. May you be wise beyond your years when you are young, and may your wisdom grow with you even into your elder years.

Alex .... We have offered you our gifts. In giving them to you, we in return have received a blessing from the experience. But, you too must give of yourself, and give back to the world some of what you receive.

Courtney .... To symbolize this, when we are finished here, I will lead you both with your bowls to the Women's Shrine where you may pour out its contents on the ground as an offering.

Ritualist A .... *This officiate invites each guest to share some personal wisdom, or some piece of advice they wish they had had at their age, with the two girls.*

Parents .... *Alex and Courtney present a book to each of the girls. In the book is advice to each of the girls from people who could not make it to the ceremony. Some passages from the books are read aloud.*

Ritualist B .... *This officiate presides over opening the circle. They give offerings to the Ancients and thanks to all beings and spirits that have attended.*

Guests .... *The same guests that called to the quarters bid a respectful farewell to their direction in their own manner.*

Ritualist A .... Welcome, Sisters, to our circle!! Our circle is open, yet unbroken.

All .... Blessed Be!!!

Everyone then processes from the Birch Grove down to Staff Camp for cakes and ale. Along the way some stop at the Women's Shrine, where newly made women are introduced to the shrine and make their first offerings there.

- - - - - - - - - - ~ - - - - - - - - - -

The day of the ceremony was hectic, stressful, joyous, and emotional. I will forever laugh at the memory of Alex stopping me en route to the Birch Grove and sitting me down for a glass of wine to calm our nerves before the ceremony. It was worth the effort it took to get me seated, but we both knew that our nerves would not be so easily settled!

We had already set up the altar earlier in the day, and our daughters' mutual friend had volunteered herself to be the girls' personal stylist and was to escort them to the Birch Grove on our cue, so there wasn't much else to do but relax for a moment. It was during that quiet moment in which the realization that our daughters were no longer going to be our little girls, but young women, sunk in.

Pass the Kleenex, please! Bittersweet and immensely proud tears started to stream down my cheeks. I laughed alongside Alex's giggle, swallowed down my last sip of wine, wiped my tears, and side-by-side we bravely made our way to the Birch Grove to see our daughters into womanhood.

The sun, we say, came out for their ceremony, as it had been overcast all morning. Our daughters were stunningly beautiful upon their entrance as girls, and even more so upon their exit as women.

We laughed, we cried, we shared stories with one another, we shared gifts of wisdom, advice, and love. We and our loved ones all gave something to Haley and Emily to aid them on their new chapter of their journeys. Each of them was presented a book in which their female family and friends had written words of wisdom, well wishes, and sentiments into for them to carry forever.

When their vessels were full with offerings, the circle was opened and the Ancestors thanked and provided offerings, the introduction of our two new Sisters was made. We then had our guests go ahead of us to Staff Camp for cakes and ale.

I then guided our daughters in silence to the Women's Shrine. It was here that they gave their offerings and were personally welcomed by myself as fellow Sisters. Being able to share that with them was a moment I will forever hold dear and never forget.

As we proudly walked with our daughters to meet our loved ones for celebrations of cakes and ale, I could hear behind us the faint laughter and singing in the gentle breeze of the birch trees' branches.

A new chapter has begun.

- - - - - - - - - - ~ - - - - - - - - - -

Alex and I could not write this out together, as we reside in two separate provinces. As elaborate as my account is for the telling of our daughters' Coming of Age Ceremony, Alex's emotional account of the event is beautiful and a must read. Alex writes:

> The Coming of Age ceremony was important for me as a way to recognize my daughter as her own person, and as a member of the community in her own right. I wanted to make sure she felt surrounded by supportive friends and mentors as she entered her teenage years so she would not feel alone. Emily had already begun to take on more adult responsibilities and I felt it was time she be recognized for the amazing person she is.
>
> It was a very emotional experience for me, recognizing that my dear child was a young woman. It still stuns me every day. And so it is hard to put to words what a ceremony like that really means. There were people there who had given me support and confidence when I didn't even know if I would make a good parent. There were people who have supported us through life's challenges, and those who have shared the joys of festival celebrations. The beauty and strength of the community and the land was reflected in our daughters, and it gave me so much joy to be able to create that with Courtney.
>
> Raven's Knoll is the place where we have built our community. Emily and I have been a part of the Knoll since the first work weekends. Having a place where everyone knows our names, where we can have our contributions valued, where we can celebrate ourselves and our friends and our values: these are gifts that we hope to share with others and keep the spirit of the people and the land alive with us wherever we go.

- - - - - - - - - - ~ - - - - - - - - - -

For those who may be considering a ceremony of this sort for your child, some friendly advice to you:

1. Social media is a beautiful tool! We used Facebook in the planning stages for guest list, idea sharing, and asking our guests if they were comfortable in taking on certain roles within the ceremony. We created

our own group page and the benefits of having everyone in-the-know were substantial. You can also sort out times, dates, location, RSVP etc.

2. Ask your child's input. They may not have a lot to say about it, but any input from them for their ceremony can be helpful towards its creation.

3. Research! Write down what you want your child to gain from such a ceremony, what is important to them, what things they will like etc. before planning how the ceremony will go. Personalize it! This is their special day after all!

4. Don't take everything on yourself! Remember, you want your child to experience this special day, but if you have too much taken on, you will miss out on seeing them experience it! If your friends and family offer to help, take them up on the offer!

5. Try not to stress too much and be prepared for the emotional aspects! Have someone bring you Kleenex! We designated Kleenex bearers for the ceremony as we are both emotional saps when it comes to our girls!

6. Set up your space beforehand. It saves time and provides less stress.

7. Ask your guests if they are comfortable in participating. Don't ever assume that they are fine with public speaking; many are not.

8. Make sure your child is aware and accepting of the ceremony aspects so they don't get overwhelmed beforehand.

9. Have fun!

10. Repeat step 9!

Endnote:

i. "Anticifest" is the weekend before, and the days leading up to, the Kaleidoscope Gathering. Over the years it has become a large social occasion in its own right.

Courtney Rheaume, affectionately known as "the Brat," has been a longtime volunteer in the Pagan communities in Montreal and in parts of Ontario. Her service has included working at children's programs, on security, at greeting, as an assistant event coordinator with the Montreal Pagan Resource Centre (MPRC), and running food services with the Raven's Knoll YAG. Courtney is known from Montreal to Raven's Knoll for her mischievous smile and laughter. (She's a ginger pirate lass. What did you expect?!) When she's not running after her teenager, you can rest assured she's in the kitchen creating a new recipe for the masses to try or planning her next adventures.

Alex Thomas is a mysterious and friendly creature of the night who loves cooking for people and making things sparkle. Alex's home is in Ottawa, and they are a long-time volunteer and friend of the Raven's Knoll community. They are a dedicated sole parent of a wonderful teen.

SONG TO THE KNOLL

by Juniper Birch

I call upon the land of Raven's Knoll
The mysterious ways of the Bonnechere River
Mysterious as the shadows of Mirkwood
Shadowed as the depths of the swamp
Deep as the waters of the Sacred Well
The joy of swimming in the waters of the Cauldron
Joyful as the dancers around the Drumming Fire Pit
Dancing as the leaves in the Birch Grove
Sticks, leaves and pine needles raked away at work weekends
Pine needles that make our beds under the pine forest
Peace and pride found under the Rainbow Tree
With honour and pride we raise God Poles in the Vé
And honour given to our Ancestors at the Standing Stone
Ancestors and lost women we remember with the great Dream Catcher
Dreams we hold dear as we kneel before the Lord and Lady Shrine
Strong women who refuse to kneel at the Red Spiral
Spiraling into the centre of the Witchring to visit the stangs there
A centre of strength and manhood at the Men's Cairn
Strong backs who keep the fires
Little fires of memory that we kindle in our hearts
Warmly we remember lost pets and loved ones together
Firelight that brings warmth and mirth
Reverence and mirth at the Trickster's pole
Mirth and song lift our spirits at the stage
Spirits of the land whom we make offerings to at Gnome Home
Offerings given as we bake in the hot sands around the berms
And eat the bread baked in the wood-fired oven that we built

Together we work to build community in the Raven Field
Ravens who fly above the knolls that guard this land
We call upon the land of Raven's Knoll
We honour our Gods
We honour the Spirits
We honour the Ancestors
Thrice hail!

Juniper Birch just happened to move to Ontario around the time that
Raven's Knoll was acquired. Since then she has volunteered her time and
effort to support the campground and many of the events that are held
there, including organizing and running The Witches' Sabbat at Raven's
Knoll. Beyond this, Juniper has run blogs and podcasts on Paganism and
witchcraft and published a variety of articles on these subjects. Juniper has
contributed to two anthologies: "To Fly by Night" published by Pendraig,
and "Hoofprints in the Wildwood" published by Gullinbursti Press.

*This page
has been
intentionally
left
fnord.*

ABOUT RAVEN'S KNOLL EVENTS

Raven's Knoll is open seasonally, from May to October. There are many gatherings and events that take place at the Knoll. A few of the regular spiritual events are outlined here. There are more scheduled opportunities for volunteers to pitch in to maintain the Knoll and build projects (called "work weekends"), which take place roughly once a month. Also, there are both periodic and regular secular events that happen at the Knoll, from weddings to historical re-enacting meet-ups to martial arts seminars to cosplay and Live Action Role-Play events. Information on Raven's Knoll and other events can be found at www.ravensknoll.ca or by joining the "Raven's Knoll" Facebook group.

Beltaine Work Weekend: The first work weekend at Raven's Knoll features a May Pole Dance and Beltaine ritual, as well as a Walpurgisnacht ritual and bonfire. Takes place on a weekend near the start of May.

Well and Tree Gathering: This open Pagan and Heathen gathering pays tribute to the impending planting season, the fertility of life, and the field. It features the annual Procession of Her Holy Mother Nerthus, a Germanic Pagan Goddess. Takes place the Victoria Day long weekend. For information see www.wellandtree.ca.

Witches' Sabbat at Raven's Knoll: The purpose of the Sabbat is to provide a forum where practitioners and other interested persons can come together to learn and share information relating to non-Wiccan witchcraft and its associated practices. The weekend consists of rituals, discussions, workshops, a potluck with stone soup feast, and much more. Together, attendees build a relationship with the land, create a stang for the main ritual, tell stories, hang out around the fire pit, and most importantly: learn, share, and grow as Witches. Each year there is a different theme and featured herb. Takes place the last weekend in May. For information see www.witchessabbat.ca.

Three Rivers Festival: The annual gathering of the Eastern Ontario members of *Ár nDraíocht Féin: A Druid Fellowship* (ADF). Everyone is welcome. Each year there is a theme related to a deity, with a ritual and oftentimes a new idol erected in the Raven's Knoll Nematon (a shrine to the Celtic Gods). Usually takes place on a weekend at the start of June. For information see www.3riversfestival.wordpress.com.

Firemonger's Workshop: This is a hands-on weekend for people interested in the art and skill of managing Pagan festival fires. This is a workshop for people who seriously want to burn things. The event also features a potluck cooked over the fire. Takes place at variable times in June or July.

Hail and Horn Gathering: This gathering brings together a diverse array of Heathens and people who practice Northern Tradition spirituality. The gathering features an elaborate blót, the raising of a God-pole in the Raven's Knoll Vé, a húsel of traditional foods, and a high symbel (sumbel). Takes place the Canada Day long weekend. For information see www.hailandhorn.ca.

AnticiFest: An informal and improvised Pagan social event that builds anticipation for Canada's largest Pagan festival, the Kaleidoscope Gathering. Takes place the weekend before, through to the end of, the Tuesday before the August long weekend.

Kaleidoscope Gathering: "KG" is Canada's largest, and second longest running, Pagan festival. It includes well over 100 scheduled workshops, concerts, rituals, ceremonies, and activities each year; including a featured main ritual on the annual theme of the festival, a Bardic Competition, evening concerts, a separate children's program, nightly drumming and dancing around the bonfire, workshops by community members, Stag King and Huntress rituals, and a Pride Parade. Takes place the Wednesday before, through to the end of, the August long weekend. For information see www.kaleidoscope-gathering.ca.

LebowskiCampFest: The Raven's Knoll congregation of the Church of the Latter-Day Dude holds an annual tent revival to learn from, and apply, the teachings of the Dude. This fest is a campout where attendees commune with the wisdom of the movie "The Big Lebowski" through the religion of Dudeism. Takes place the second weekend in August. For information see the Facebook page for "LebowskiCampFest."

Pagans Unplugged: This is a simple camping excursion for Pagans, without being plugged in to phones, computers, and worries. There is no programming, just hanging out with friends doing regular stuff at the Knoll such as swimming, bonfires, stargazing, hammock-napping, archery, wandering, and more. (It is not a music event, but people are free to make music.) Takes place the Labour Day long weekend.

KornuKopia Gathering: This gathering is for Pagans, Heathens, and their friends to celebrate the last bounty of the summer and the turning of the Wheel of the Year into fall, honouring the Gods in mirth and reverence. The festival features the burning of the Man in sacrifice to the Goddess on behalf of the folk, workshops by community members, a preserves competition, chanting and singing around the campfire, and a communal fall fruits feast. Takes place on the weekend closest to September 19 (which is Talk Like a Pirate Day and the anniversary of the founding of Raven's Knoll). For information see the Facebook page for "KornuKopia Gathering."

Closing Work Weekend: The last work weekend at Raven's Knoll features an ecumenical sumbel (symbel) ritual. Takes place on a weekend near the end of October.

ABOUT THE EDITORS

Juniper Birch just happened to move to Ontario around the time that Raven's Knoll was acquired. Since then she has volunteered her time and effort to support the campground and many of the events that are held there, including organizing and running The Witches' Sabbat at Raven's Knoll. Beyond this, Juniper has run blogs and podcasts on Paganism and witchcraft and published a variety of articles on these subjects. Juniper has contributed to two anthologies: "To Fly by Night" published by Pendraig, and "Hoofprints in the Wildwood" published by Gullinbursti Press.

Austin Lawrence is known in the Pagan community as "Auz." He is one of the Stewards of Raven's Knoll and a co-organizer of the Kaleidoscope Gathering. Auz has a Master's degree in Anthropology and is a Heathen who is an oathed Goði that serves as the Keeper of the Raven's Knoll Vé. Auz is also a former Stag King of the Kaleidoscope Gathering. He lives in Ottawa with his wife Maryanne Pearce, his two adult children Kadri Rainne and Joven Wolf, and a menagerie of family pets.

Gypsy Birch is a member of Raven's Knoll staff, performing such duties as security and maintenance, as well as assists in organization for multiple events. He is also part of the Flying Monkey security team for the Kaleidoscope Gathering. While he has no defined personal practice pertaining to a particular spiritual path, Gypsy assists followers of many different faiths to ensure that their event or ritual meets the logistical needs of the organizers and attendees.

Maryanne Pearce, also known as MA, is one of the Stewards of Raven's Knoll and a co-organizer of the Kaleidoscope Gathering. She holds a doctorate in law, focusing on missing and murdered vulnerable women. Her Master's thesis in Anthropology focused on the Canadian Pagan community. MA is in charge of all the paper involved with RK and KG. She lives in Ottawa with her husband Austin Lawrence, her two adult children Kadri Rainne and Joven Wolf, and various four legged friends.

Printed in Great Britain
by Amazon